Imperfect World . . . Perfect Me!

Imperfect World . . . Perfect Me!

A guide to living Christlike in a world that isn't

Karen Ayers

Foreword by Pastor Karen Smith

Strategic Book Publishing and Rights Co.

Strategic Book Publishing & Rights Co., LLC
USA | Singapore
www.sbpra.com

ISBN: 978-1-68181-697-5

To Jim, my husband.

Thank you for obeying the Holy Spirit and asking me to marry you. I'm excited to see what the future holds for us. Both of us know that to make a marriage great we must put God first. I truly love you; my prayer partner.

****

To Ken, my investor and friend. Thank you for believing in me and encouraging me to write.

****

To our children: Megan, Angela, Jennifer, Kristopher, Mary, Whitney, Heather, Brandon, Lance and Jordan.

My prayer for each of you is that you understand what a true relationship with Jesus Christ truly is and strive to live Christlike every day. Forgive me for the times I let you down and didn't live so Christlike myself.

****

To Pastor Karen Smith, my teacher and friend.

There are no words to describe what you mean to me. The knowledge you have placed inside of me is one of my most precious gifts. You are my mentor. A true example of what living Christlike really is. Thank you for leading by example.

****

But most of all, I thank Jesus Christ for wrapping me in His loving arms and loving me even when I didn't deserve to be loved. You saved my soul and forgave me by Your grace and mercy. To You I owe EVERYTHING and also because of You, I have hope and a future.

Foreword

****

"Karen's book is sincere, honest, and transparent. She has been through difficult times, but she points the reader to Jesus – "the Author and Finisher of our faith." She shares her heart's struggles in ways that equip the lives of others!"

Cindy C. Sherrill. Ed. S.
University Professor of Teacher Education

****

"There are times in our lives that we regret and wish there had been a guide to avoiding at least a few of the blunders we stumble into, much less the ones we blatantly jumped into. Karen, (the most amazing wife on the planet) lives her life the way she writes it.... wide open and without a parachute. She will bring you into her life and make you cry and lift you up. She is a poignant writer and not pretentious in writing or in person. This book is a pathway to the young and old in faith. I have never read a self-help book I couldn't put down until now. I have been a born-again Christian for almost 50 years now, and this book brought true tears to my eyes with its honesty and conviction of who I have not been and should have been all along. She is an amazing woman, with an amazing

story to tell, with real answers to life's most difficult questions and I am proud to call her wife, friend and mother. She captures the real need to be who we say we are, and opens your eyes to the heart to see the path.

Enjoy reading her book and see where your heart ends up at the end of this amazing journey you're about to undertake. Well done sweetheart......well done indeed! May I learn to walk as you do by your example you live out in front of me."

James (Jim) McKee
Husband, Friend, Father, Business Owner

****

Imperfect World . . . Perfect Me! is more than just a guide to help you become a better Christian, it is from start to finish a journey that pulls you closer to Christ. As you read, you will distinctly feel as though you are sitting down with a new dear friend, as she shares the difference her dear friends, the Father, the Son Jesus, and the Holy Spirit have made in her life. Karen Ayers has such a beautiful love walk with the Lord that everyone she meets quickly sees that there is just something very precious about her. So, grab a cup of coffee and as you open these pages, let her warmth, honesty, and genuine faith inspire and fuel your passion to know and trust Him more deeply than ever before!

Pastor Wanda Atkins
Outreach Evangelism Coordinator
Christ Fellowship Church
Dawsonville, Georgia

****

"When Karen asked me to read over her latest book, I was excited and intrigued. She writes with such passion that I am always excited to read what she has written, but she warned me that this book was different from anything she had ever done.....and it is.

She always weaves God and His works into the stories she creates and builds characters who struggle to find Him and walk with Him through, and in spite of, adversities and temptations in their lives. This book, however, goes beyond fiction to embrace the struggles of real people, including those of Karen and her husband, Jim, as well as those of other people whose lives have touched theirs.

It is heartbreaking at times, but greatly uplifting as well. She tackles what it means to be a Christian, the importance of finding a good church, and the many facets of truly living a life close to Christ, including forgiving yourself and others and letting go of habits and people who are spiritually toxic to you.

Karen has been a friend to our family for many years, beginning with our daughters forming a close friendship that continues to this day. I taught her son, and she took care of my grandson. She has allowed me the privilege of serving as her editor for many of her books, granting me a rare glimpse into the fascinating process involved in the creation of a book.

I was a part of her life during some of the personal struggles she details in this book, and it breaks my heart that I did not realize at the time just how much she was struggling. But God is good. He brought her through those very dark hours and remains by her side, on the path ahead, and within her – an Ever-present Helper, which is really what this book is all about. I am honored to have had a tiny part in helping it come about – enjoy!"

Lorri Mincey
Teacher, Editor, Friend

*****

Imperfect World . . . Perfect Me! is a step-by-step handbook to living the full life that is found only in Jesus Christ. In her transparency, Karen shares her testimony regarding some of her own personal struggles. She explains how she overcame the obstacles each situation presented by trusting God, applying His Word, and knowing her identity in Christ.

Karen covers everything from having a personal relationship with Jesus to marriage to self-esteem, and gives encouraging truths from God's Word that will move you from a mindset of defeat to a mindset of faith, all rooted in the promises of God.

Imperfect World . . . Perfect Me! is one of those books that won't leave your nightstand – a quick reference that is power-packed with inspiration from someone who has walked some tough paths in her life! You will enjoy Karen's work and you will fall in love with her faith to simply believe what God says about you!

Pastor Karen Smith
President, KINEO Ministry Training Center
Christ Fellowship Church
Dawsonville, Georgia

Introduction

Never in a million years did I ever fathom that I would be writing a self-help book. As an author of Christian fiction and motivational speaker, I love making up stories of the lives of fictional characters and how they overcome struggles with Christ, but a true-to-life book? No, not me.

Of course, our plans are not always God's plans, and as I was struggling to write my seventh Christian Fiction book, the Holy Spirit starting guiding me in another direction-- pulling me away from fiction and toward something I found myself terrified with.

Nonfiction is only frightening because it must be accurate. Was I ready for such a big feat? The Holy Spirit seemed to think I was.

So many nights I couldn't sleep as He poured into me what were to be the pages in this book, His book, for He was the inspiration; I was merely the hands.

He showed me that my own struggles and experiences made me stronger and must be shared. In fact, some He allowed me to go through so I might be a blessing to others.

My prayer for you is that this book touches you, whether it is a certain chapter or its entirety.

It's easy to ***say*** you are a Christian, but are you truly living a Christlike life that is pleasing to God?

As we make our way through chapter after chapter, you will be pulled closer to His glorious presence and what He desires for you in your life.

Imperfect World . . . Perfect Me! will lead you down the road to living more Christlike--and I'm excited to travel the road with you.

It is crucial that you realize the Bible is the living, breathing Word of God. If for some reason you don't believe this, then this book will be of no help to you, as it is full of God's Word.

If there is one thing I have learned in over fifty years on this earth, you cannot find true joy without God, and His Word is the only thing that can lead you there.

It upsets me when people say, "How can you believe in a book that has been translated and changed so many times?"

But the truth is, the Bible was only translated from Hebrew to English in the Old Testament and from Greek to English in the New Testament. Sure, there are different versions that might be a bit easier to understand, but they all mean and basically say the same thing, just worded a little differently. I choose to read an NIV Bible. I find it more like the King James than any other. I love my Bible, even though some of the pages are falling out and I have written all over it, taking notes that mean something to me, notes that I go back to often and reread, notes that my children will read someday when I'm gone and know how much their momma truly loved Jesus.

Another thing that is important before we start the first chapter is that reading a book that will show you how to live more Christlike, you must first have Him living inside.

Being a Christian isn't just believing that Jesus is your Savior, the Son of God, and God in the flesh. It's asking Him into your life after confessing your sins and repenting. I once heard it said that being in a garage doesn't make you a car, any more than being in a church makes you a Christian.

But one more thing before we start--something I want you to think about. If you were on trial for being a Christian, would there be enough evidence to convict you?

Chapter One

Will the REAL Christian please stand up!

****

Therefore if anyone is in Christ, he is a new creation. The old has passed away; behold the new has come. *(2 Corinthians 5:17) NIV*

****

I trust that if you have picked up this book as a guide to living more Christlike, you are already a Christian. Or perhaps someone who cares about you placed it in your hands so that you might be blessed. Maybe you're going through a hard period in your life. In either case, it's okay.

In this chapter, I will explain what being a ***Christian*** really means.

****

Some think it is only believing in Jesus Christ. Believing that He was born of a virgin and lived and died on this earth for our sins and rose again after just three days. Some believe that having been raised in church and continuing to attend on a weekly basis makes them a Christian.

Some think that living a life as best they can, with no deliberate sin, being good to others, and paying tithes faithfully makes them a Christian.

And believe it or not, some even think that doing mission work, pastoring a church, becoming a Sunday school teacher, writing Christian books, or being involved in any sort of Christian work obviously makes them a Christian.

All these things are great indeed, but absolutely none of them make you a Christian.

****

Not everyone who says to Me, 'Lord, Lord,' will enter the kingdom of heaven, but only he who does the will of My Father who is in heaven. Many will say to Me on that day, 'Lord, Lord, did we not prophesy in Your name, and in Your name drive out demons and perform many miracles? Then I will tell them plainly, 'I never knew you. Away from Me you evildoers!' *(Matthew 7:21-23) NIV*

****

Sadly, many who call themselves Christians really aren't Christians at all. What's even worse is they honestly believe they are.

In truth, if you have read this far and are now asking yourself, exactly what makes me a Christian, you are probably in one of the groups I mentioned above.

So now you might be thinking.....Are you serious? All my life I thought I was a Christian. I was raised in church and never missed a Sunday. I've believed in Jesus Christ all of my life! Why would Jesus ***ever*** turn me away?

But just as Matthew 7:21-23 says, many will stand before God and call out all the things they did, and Jesus will say, "Depart from Me, I never knew you."

So how do you ***know*** Christ?

When Jesus told Nicodemus that the only way to heaven was to be born again, Nicodemus became confused and asked, "How can a man be born again when he is old? Surely he cannot enter a second time into his mother's womb?"

Jesus answered and said,

"I tell you the truth; no one can see the kingdom of heaven unless he is born again." *(John3:3) NIV*

So just how do you become ***born-again***, or ***saved*** as many call it?

****

If you confess with your mouth, "Jesus is Lord," and believe in your heart that God raised Him from the dead, you will be saved. *(Romans 10:9)NIV*

****

And another:

Everyone who calls on the name of the Lord will be saved. *(Romans 10:13)NIV*

****

And my favorite verse:

For God so loved the world, that He gave His only begotten Son, that whosoever believeth in Him, shall not perish but have ever lasting life. *(John 3:16) KJV*

****

Being ***born-again*** is simple really, and because it is so simple many fail to see the simplicity of it.

Many denominations think the only way to heaven is by your works; that if we don't do ***enough*** we will never make the mark. But this simply isn't true.

****

For it is by grace you have been saved, through faith, and this not from yourselves, it is the gift of God, not by works, so that no one can boast. *(Ephesians 2:8-9)NIV*

****

I was saved when I was eleven years old. I was raised in a Baptist church, and on that particular day, I remember Mr. Bryant preaching on hell and what I needed to do in order to escape the hot flames that would forever torment me throughout eternity.

I only remember bits and pieces of his sermon on that long ago day, but I do remember the way I felt. Even though I was only eleven years old, the tug on my heart was heavy. The longing I had to be one with Jesus was real, and I knew He was calling me to be saved.

Keep in mind, though, that I was an extremely shy eleven-year-old who was tall and skinny and who felt extremely ugly, and nothing anyone could do or say would make my feet move toward the front of the church on that particular Sunday morning. After all, what would everyone think of me? They would actually ***know*** that I had not yet been saved, and to me that was quite embarrassing.

Later that night (after a full day of feeling guilty) I found my mother in the kitchen doing dishes.

"Momma, can a person be saved at home, or do they have to be in church?"

Momma looked at me in wonder. I think she knew I was ready. "Of course they can. All you have to do is ask Jesus into your heart, believe that He was the Son of God and died for us, and that He rose again."

"So if I ask Him to save me, then I will be saved?"

I was very curious and I did not want to mess this up. After all, my salvation was at stake, right? I didn't want to die and go to the fiery hell I had heard our pastor speak of.

I remember Momma smiling. "Would you like for me to pray with you?"

"No, not now, but thanks."

I often wonder why I didn't get my momma to pray with me that night. Not sure if I was too shy even for her, or if I really just wanted to do this on my own, just Jesus and myself.

I had been having visions since I was five years old and journaling since the age of seven or eight. I have known I wanted to be a writer since the age of nine, and I also knew that I was a ***'little different'*** from others; perhaps only because I was introverted and withdrawn.

I said my prayers nightly when I was very young. I said.... "Now I lay me down to sleep, I pray the Lord my soul to keep, if I should die before I wake, I pray the Lord my soul to take."

As I became older I learned the Lord's Prayer and that was my prayer each night, but never had I truly poured my heart out to God until that night in 1976.

All day the Lord had called to me, and when bedtime finally came and I found myself alone, I felt guilty for not going up in church that day. I first asked Jesus to forgive me for being shy, and I told Him how much I loved Him. I told Him that I believed He was the Son of God and that He died for my sins, so that I might live. It was the first time I had ever been on my knees.

I can remember as I spoke something strange started to happen; something that I had never experienced before. My body became as light as a feather, and I felt as if I was floating. I know now it was the Holy Spirit. He was everywhere and He was happy I was inviting Him in.

Now at fifty-one, I look back and realize I haven't lived a perfect life. So many times I missed the mark or fell short. So many times I did things that were displeasing to God. Things I am completely ashamed of.

But I do know this….never once did He ever leave me since that night in 1976. He has continued to love me even when I wasn't lovable.

****

Be strong and courageous. Do not be afraid or terrified because of them, for the Lord your God goes with you; He will never leave you nor forsake you. *(Deuteronomy 31:6) NIV*

****

Not so long ago a nurse at the hospital started telling me how hard it was to get to heaven. She believed that our sin would keep us from going to that glorious place even ***after*** we ask Jesus into our life.

She believed that Jesus would strike our name from the book of life.

The truth is our name is in the book of life before we are ever born and the only way it will be erased is if we die before we have been born again. It really is that easy!

****

My husband Jim is allowing me to share his salvation story. I wanted to share it because it is very different from mine, just as are so many I have listened to over the years.

Jesus calls to us at all ages, and for Jim it was when he was only six years old. Some may think a child that young has no idea what being saved ***really*** means, but I have found that is not true. Children are innocent and with God even before they were born, so why wouldn't they be able to feel His presence?

Jim lived in Miami, Florida, where there was much drug crime, in the sixties. He had been molested off and on since the age of three, and by six years of age knew more than most children his age. His parents raised him in church and he had heard about God.

As Jim sat at the swing set in the back yard of his Miami home, looking out at the canal and palm trees, he questioned God, asking if He was real. He knew in his young heart that if God truly was real, then he needed His help in order for him to survive the abuse from babysitters and neighbors.

In Jim's young mind, he wasn't exactly sure at that time if God was real, so he asked God to help him and show him that He was real and not just some made-up fairy tale. Like most curious boys, he needed proof.

He enjoyed explaining to me how wonderful it felt. He said he became light, as if he were floating. I understood, for I had experienced the same thing; that peaceful feeling that can come only from God.

Even at six, he understood that he was feeling the presence of God. He asked Jesus that day to save him and vowed to live for Him all the days of his life.

Now fast forward a week later, when Jim was walking his daily half-mile home from school.

Satan was at work, telling his young mind that God wasn't real, even after he had experienced His presence. He again questioned God. (Knowing my husband, I can see him doing this.)

It was starting to rain, and Jim said aloud, "God, if you are real, keep it from raining on me so I won't get wet." He was afraid that if his school books became damp, he would get in trouble by his parents, who were very strict.

It started to rain across the street and kept raining all around him on his journey home, but never once did a drop hit Jim.

As he made it safely inside his home and shut the door, the sky began to downpour. Never, since that day, has Jim questioned the existence of God again.

****

Seriously, there are no magic words that make you a Christian. It is simply the tug of God and the desire of your heart to confess your sins and repent; to step into that place where you know that you know that you are ready to be born again. To leave the old behind and become a new creation in Christ.

If you have never invited Jesus into your life, then there is no better time than the present. It's easy to think there will always be time later, but the truth is, we are never promised tomorrow. With the world growing less Christlike daily, and horror on every corner of the globe, it's dangerous to live without Christ, for each day could be our last.

Ask yourself, are you ready? I mean ***really*** ready? Have you invited Him in, or did you take your Christianity for granted, assuming you were a Christian all along?

If you can't remember the day you prayed the prayer of salvation and humbled yourself before a loving God, chances are you do not have a blood covenant with Jesus.

Maybe you have already been feeling God calling you, inviting you to come to Him, to trust in Him and allow Him to guide you through the rest of your life. Trust me; it's much easier with the Holy Spirit living within than without Him at all.

Man's darkest hour is when he refuses the invitation to come to God.

Pastor Todd Smith

****

As you start the next chapter and the chapters hereafter, you will be shown how to live more Christlike, but you first must ***know*** you are truly a Christian and that the Holy Spirit, in fact, dwells within you.

I've written out the prayer of salvation to help you. As I said, there are no magical words; it is mostly just confessing and believing with your heart and inviting Him inside. Jesus will not come where He is not invited.

****

Dear Lord....I believe that You are the Son of God. I believe that You came to this earth and died for my sins. I am asking You today to fill my mind, body and soul with Your Holy presence, and save me from this dying world. Forgive me, Lord, from past sins and wash me clean. Today dear Jesus, wipe the slate clean and allow me to start over, a new creation in You, and You in me. Thank You, Lord Jesus, for saving me! Amen!

****

But remember it's not just saying the words, but truly feeling the words you speak. You will ***know*** it, because you will ***feel*** it, and you will never doubt your salvation.

It's a scary thought to go through life without God. Once you have invited Him to dwell within you, you then have a blood covenant with Jesus and nothing, and I mean nothing, will separate you from Him.

Now, let's begin again our journey as true Christians and see where God leads us.

Chapter Two

Being Comfortable In Your Own Skin.

****

You are beautiful, for you are fearfully and wonderfully made. *(Psalm 139:14) NIV*

****

It wasn't so long ago I was the one needing this chapter.

I grew up feeling like an ugly duckling.

I was comfortable around my cousins and very close friends, because I knew them so well, but strangers were another story. I would never look anyone in the eyes when I spoke, because I didn't want them to concentrate too long on my face and see how ugly I was.

Through high school you could count my friends on one hand. I was bullied and called names. I knew it was because I was ugly, and I never understood why God made some so beautiful and me so unappealing.

You see, when I was five years old, I stood on my tiptoes at Habersham County Hospital holding my daddy's hand as I peered into the window at my brand-new baby sister. I remember the day as if it were yesterday, for it's actually the first memory I remember at all.

A woman walked up and told my daddy that my baby sister was the most beautiful baby she had ever laid eyes on.

My daddy thanked her and then said, "This one here was the ugliest baby ever born." And he proceeded to move back so she could take a closer look at me.

From that moment on, I shut down. I don't remember anything else my daddy said to her. Everything I believed up until that time was gone. In my mind, if my Daddy thought I was ugly, then how could he love me? Had he just been pretending to love me as he read me bedtime stories at night?

My daddy, who I loved and adored, thought I was the ugliest baby that was ever born, and not only that, he voiced it to a perfect stranger. What sort of father did that?

Because of what I heard him say that day, I walked through my life with my head down. I loved God, but I didn't understand why He hated me and made me the ugliest. After all, it was apparent that I had the face even a parent couldn't love.

Each time I looked into the mirror, all I saw was ugliness. Never once did I feel beautiful. If someone told me I was beautiful, I thought they were lying. How could they possibly see beauty in the ugliest baby ever born?

It wasn't until I was grown and on my third marriage that my daddy looked at me one day as I was working outside on one of his visits.

"You are a beautiful woman. Sometimes I don't think you realize just how beautiful you are," he said, smiling at me.

I froze. Why on earth would he tell me this? I was forty-four years old and had ***never*** been beautiful. Had he forgotten about the day I was born?

"No I'm not, Daddy. I was the ugliest baby ever born, remember? You said so yourself."

Daddy looked at me, confused. "What are you talking about?"

"Don't you remember the day Connie was born and we peered into the glass window at her? A stranger said she was the most beautiful baby, and you told her that I had been the ugliest."

Daddy looked at me for a moment, and then it was as if a light bulb came on. "Oh, Yvonne, (my parents always called me by my middle name) did you not listen to everything I told her?"

"Yes, you told her how ugly I was. I remember it very well." I had waited thirty-nine years to confront my daddy with this. Thirty-nine years of resentment and hurt. Thirty-nine years of pain.

"On the night you were born, your momma had a terrible time. The delivery was awful, and she pushed and pushed but you wouldn't come. They used forceps to pull you out, and because of that your little head was so misshapen it scared us. The doctor assured us that it would take several days for your head to be the way it should be, and that you were perfectly fine. If you had listened to the whole conversation, you would have heard me tell her to just look at you now. Look at how beautiful you were. I've always thought you were beautiful."

I dropped my shovel and stood looking at him. Had I really gone thirty-nine years of my life feeling ugly, when my daddy actually thought I was beautiful? How might my life have been different had I thought I was beautiful?

So many times in life we let something someone else says, or something we ***think*** they said about us, define who we are and what we think about ourselves.

Sometimes people can be cruel and say the most hurtful things, but the truth is, God made us in His image; therefore, how could we possibly be anything else but beautiful?

My daddy said I was ugly, so I became ugly in my mind. Each time anyone bragged on me in the years after, my mind immediately went back to that October day in 1970, and I replayed the entire scene in my head.

Had I listened to the entire conversation between him and a stranger and heard that he actually thought I was beautiful, my entire life would have been different. Instead of being shy and withdrawn, I would have been outspoken and bold with confidence.

It is so important for us not to listen to the opinion of others when it comes to our looks. It is also important for you to tell your children daily that they are beautiful, so they grow up with confidence.

Why would God create junk? He doesn't make mistakes; therefore, to God we are all beautiful. If God doesn't make mistakes, then He couldn't possibly have made a mistake with you.

****

God created man in His own image, in the image of God He created him; male and female, He created them. *(Genesis 1:27) NIV*

****

Being comfortable in your own skin is extremely hard for most of us. Now, when I look in the mirror, I see a bold woman to whom God has given confidence.

I see that I am a child of God, a princess my heavenly Father loves and adores.

And I'd be lying to you if I said I never observe the wrinkles that keep taking up residence on my face, or the extra weight that makes my pants fit tighter. Sometimes I get disgusted with myself for allowing the weight to creep up. But never again will I feel ugly, for to say I am ugly would be to put down my Father who created me in His image, out of the love that only He can give.

When we look at our children, we don't see flaws; we only see the beautiful people we helped to create by our DNA. And God doesn't see flaws in our appearance. To God, He couldn't have made us more beautiful. We look exactly the way He created us to look.

But let's face it, if we don't love ourselves, how can we ever expect anyone else to? I'm sure each morning when you look at your reflection staring back, you can find a hundred things you would like to change.

Maybe you are overweight or struggle with being underweight. Maybe your wrinkles are more noticeable and gray hairs are showing, or your hair is thinning at the speed of light as my own hair seems to be doing these days. But truly, what does it matter? Some things we can change and some things we can't, and we cannot beat ourselves up over the things we have no control over.

You are your own worst enemy. I've been my own most of my life. Only now I know I am beautiful. I may not look as beautiful on the outside as some, but I strive to do the best with what God has given me. And because God thinks I am, then I must be.

I am beautiful because I was created by God, and He loves me just as I am.

I keep my hair dyed and styled, wear makeup to cover up the now-appearing age spots, and try to dress as best I can. (I love Goodwill shopping.)

When we feel good about ourselves, then it reflects how we act or how we project ourselves to others.

Have you ever rushed out feeling you looked your worst, hoping that you wouldn't run into someone you knew, and sure enough, around the corner at Walmart was someone you'd known for years? And here you were--hair a mess and no makeup.

You tried to be friendly, but in all honesty you wanted to run and hide. If you're like me, you might even have made an excuse as to why you looked so terrible. (I smile as I write this because I have done this so many times.)

****

My husband is bald, and I think he is adorable. I always tell him that God made a few perfect men, and the rest he covered with hair.

When he was fifteen, back before he lost his hair, it was carrot orange. Everyone nicknamed him Opie, after Opie Taylor from The Andy Griffith Show back in the sixties.

One day he was in shop class as a freshman in high school, sitting in front of two girls, when one dropped something.

Jim was taught to be a gentleman and leaned down to pick it up for her. As he was picking it up, he felt a very hard blow to his head. Just as his teacher was walking into the room, the girl hit him on the back of the head with a hammer.

"Why did you do that?" the teacher yelled.

"Because his hair is ugly; I hate his ugly hair!"

Jim already suffered from a very low self-esteem as the only student at Miami Killian High School who had been born with bright red hair and pale skin, and to be hit on the head with a hammer and called ugly made it even worse.

Still, to this day, he struggles with his looks, and because I know this, I make a point to tell him often that I think he is gorgeous. I love him just the way he is.

****

My point is, because of my daddy and a student at Jim's school, we went through life allowing what someone said to us make us feel ugly, when that is not pleasing to God.

To put yourself down is to put God down, since you are His creation. It's like telling God that He isn't perfect; that He made a mistake. And since God can't possibly make a mistake, we need to see ourselves as He sees us, and that is beautifully and wonderfully made.

It is so important to hold your head up and carry yourself proud.

How can people see God in us if we hang our head and proceed through life with a low self-esteem? We are God's temple that He works through for His purpose.

With each new day, our prayer should be that God use us for His glory, and in order for Him to do that, we have to carry ourselves in a Godly way, with compassion and kindness, feeling confident and beautiful.

As a Christian, the Holy Spirit lives inside of us and loves every opportunity to reach out to others through us. So maybe it's time to start looking at yourself as God does, even if you have to take a dry-erase marker and write on your mirror:

I am bold, confident and beautiful. God doesn't make mistakes, and He didn't make one with me!

Start telling yourself this daily, several times a day if you have to until you start believing it. Put little notes to yourself everywhere you will see them.

You have so much to offer the world, in your attitude, your smile, and your willingness to love others as Jesus loves.

You are beautiful and confident.

You matter.

You are special to God.

You are bold and courageous.

Chapter Three

Let Go and Let God

****

Therefore do not worry about tomorrow, for tomorrow will worry about itself. Each day has enough troubles of its own. *(Matthew 6:34)NIV*

****

When Jesus preached to the multitude, He commanded them not to worry. He knew that there would be troubles with each new day, but we were not to worry over them.

****

Therefore I tell you do not worry about your life, what you will eat or drink; or about your body, what you will wear. Is not life more important than food, and the body more important than clothes? Look at the birds of the air; they do not sow or reap or store away in barns, and yet your heavenly Father feeds them. Are you not much more valuable than they? Who by worrying can add a single hour to his life?

And why do you worry about clothes? See how the lilies of the field grow. They do not labor or spin. Yet I tell you that not even

Solomon in all his splendor was dressed like one of these. If that is how God clothes the grass of the field, which is here today and tomorrow is thrown into the fire, will He not much more clothe you. O you of little faith? So do not worry saying, 'What shall we eat?' or 'What shall we drink?' or 'What shall we wear?' For the pagans run after all these things, and your heavenly Father knows that you need them. But seek ye first His Kingdom and His righteousness, and all these things will be given to you as well. *(Matthew 6: 25-33)NIV*

****

Over and over, Jesus tells us not to worry about what we eat or drink or what we wear. And for most of us, those things are the least of our worries. In fact, those are the things most take for granted each day.

Unless you are homeless or recently lost your job, what you eat or drink or the clothes you wear is not something you ever really think about.

Instead, the worries of today concerning how to provide for your family, like paying the mortgage, car payment, and utilities.

We worry about making our spouse and children happy.

We worry about our looks and what people think about us.

We worry about our job and how to climb the ladder to success.

We worry about schoolwork and how to pay for college.

We worry about our health and the health of our loved ones.

We worry about relationships.

We worry about whether or not we are good enough and stress when we fail.

We worry about not being able to trust the people we love most.

We worry about our age, our weight, our hair.

We worry that we don't fit in.

We worry that no one cares and suffer from loneliness or depression.

We worry about our children hanging with the wrong crowd.

And the list goes on and on. What Jesus was trying to say is that if God can take care of a bird, how much more will He take care of you? And as Jesus said, how does worry add a single hour to your life?

Yet we all worry over something; some a great deal more than others.

****

When my youngest son was only nine years old, his father and I were living with my in-laws. I look back now and recall it being one of the lowest times of my life.

My ex-husband was addicted to pain medication due to health-related issues and had been for several years at this time. Because of his addiction and lack of work, we lost everything material-wise, and being unable to pay rent, we had no other choice but to live with his parents.

I was working as a nanny making only two hundred dollars a week, and he spent his time in bed suffering from withdrawals and depression. It was hard for him to cope with the reality of what he had allowed himself to lose, and so it was easier for him to feel the numbness the pain medication offered.

Our once-wonderful marriage was terrible, and I had no idea what to do next.

One day he approached me and told me he was getting a divorce.

Most women who were living the life I was living might have jumped up and down and yelled with excitement, but not me. I was devastated, hurt and betrayed.

I loved my husband with all my heart and begged him to seek help for his addiction, but he never saw himself as having a problem, and now this. After all this time of marriage, he wanted to call it quits and move on, as if I were the problem.

I won't bother you with the details of how we managed to get to this point, but the truth is I didn't know another way of life. Even though I was miserable in my marriage because of his addiction, I couldn't see myself being any other way. I just continued to hope and pray he would get help, and we would once again own our own home away from his parents and be happy.

Since nothing I could do or say would change his mind about the divorce, he moved out of his parents' home and in with a female friend of mine.

He told me that our son and I would need to also move out of his parents' home and to a place of our own, yet he gave me no financial help on getting there. He had been out of work for so long he was penniless.

Talk about worry. Here I was living on eight hundred dollars a month and was now a single mom needing a place to stay.

An acquaintance of mine found out through Facebook that we were looking for a place and offered to show me a duplex that she and her husband rented. I jumped at the chance to take a look.

My heart sank as I looked at the tiny duplex that evening. Even though it was two bedrooms, it was old and about the size of a two-car garage. She told me that it would be mine for only four hundred dollars a month, with no money down and I could have two months before the first payment was due. I took it, of course, for I had no other options and was thrilled God had blessed us through others.

I learned that day that God doesn't always give us what we want, but what we need, and certainly what we can afford. He was looking out for me, and I was grateful.

In a way, I was relieved that we had a place of our own, even though it was nothing we were used to, and with God, I made it work.

During the next three months I, along with my son, sank into a depression. Our entire world had changed and neither of us knew how to act without the man who had been such a part of our life--my husband and my son's father.

My son was able to see his dad every weekend if he wished, but the child support came to an abrupt stop when the divorce was final and he married the woman he had moved in with.

I found myself crying daily, thinking about the past and the way we had all been such a close family. Back before the pain pills, when all my children were still young enough to live at home.

Now here I was, forty-six years old, alone with my youngest son, and wondering who I was other than his mom. Did I really matter? Why would my ex-husband want to leave me? What did I do wrong? So many unanswered questions eating me up inside.

Thank God I had my son, because if it weren't for him, I am not sure what I might have done, for I am sure my emotional state would have been far worse.

I would smile to people all through the day and tell them I was fine, but deep inside I was in total turmoil. Only my son saw me break down and lose it, time after time. For no reason, something would trigger a memory and I would cry uncontrollably.

It wasn't fair. Life wasn't fair, and I questioned God daily.

I was cooking one night, food I had bought with food stamps, and my son came to me and said, "I love you, Momma."

I smiled the first smile I could muster all day and said, "I love you, too."

He looked at me with such concern in his young eyes, and I could tell he wanted to say more.

"Is something wrong?" I asked.

"I don't want to live anymore."

I rushed to him and put my arms around him. How could my once-jolly son not want to live anymore? Could he possibly feel as depressed as I felt?

With tears in my eyes I asked, "What can I do to make it better?"

"Please don't make me go back to school." He had been getting off the bus many days crying. I felt in my heart he was being bullied. The boy who used to love school in elementary now hated to get out of the car each morning in middle school.

Not only was he being bullied in school, but he had gone from a huge beautiful home filled with his sisters and brother, who were all now grown, and a father who used to do everything with him, to now only being able to see him on weekends. He had witnessed us losing our home and moving in with his grandparents and now this. Everyone had moved away. All he had was me, and all I did was cry all the time in front of him.

My son had lost his joy--his reason to want to live, and it was ***my*** fault. How could I not have seen this coming?

I vowed that night never to cry in front of him again. I prayed for God's forgiveness and asked that He also help me find my own joy as I helped my son. Joy was not something I had felt in a very long time.

The next morning, I withdrew my son from school and registered him for classes online. I wasn't sure if that was the best move for him, but I knew I had to do something drastic, and this is what I felt led to do in my spirit.

I started doing more things with him, like taking his bike each day to the park and walking while he rode.

I had such little money that I couldn't afford to buy him a hamburger off the dollar menu at McDonald's, but we made the best of what we had and found things to do that didn't cost anything.

I started taking him with me where I worked as a nanny and helping him do his school work as best I could. There was just one problem. Even though he seemed to be doing much better, I was still a mess.

I still cried myself to sleep each night and felt such resentment for my ex-husband and friend who were now married and seemed to be happy.

One day when I found myself at home alone, I paced the floors and cried out to God, Why? Why had He forsaken me? Why had He allowed me to sink so low? Could He not see me struggling to survive? Did He even love me at all?

I realize now that my thinking was selfish. God had not caused my ex to become an addict or leave me. He was not the one who took away my joy. It wasn't God who distanced Himself from me, but rather it was me who distanced myself from Him.

I fell to my knees at my coffee table and gave it all to God that day. I knew I could no longer make it on my own. I was tired of trying to do everything my way and had been a Christian long enough that I understood what I needed to do; the only thing left to do.

Peace flooded me as I cried out to God, and the Holy Spirit who had been with me all along brought back to my attention the visions I had experienced as a child and my dream of becoming a writer.

At forty-six, I had not thought of those long-ago visions in years.....me standing in front of hundreds of people speaking about God. I had tucked them away long ago, knowing I was much too shy to ever do such a thing, but now? Was I still too shy, and was this what God wanted of me?

Since the age of nine, I had dreamed of being a published author—ever since Mrs. Rogers told me in fourth grade that my short story was wonderful, and that one day I would make a great author writing fiction books.

Why now had the Holy Spirit brought all this back to me? Wasn't I too old, and how would I get started? I was poor, and the only education I had was high school.

I got up and made my way to my computer and pulled up the book I had worked on for years off and on. "Is this it? Is this what You want of me?"

I promised that if I was able to get a book published, I would use my writing for Him and I would not be afraid to speak up and tell others.

This was the day I knew I could no longer be introverted and shy. I was asking for my joy back, and I knew the only way to achieve that would be to place God first and live my life more Christlike.

I had to let go of the pain and hurt of my ex-husband and friend and forgive them.

Did I suddenly become perfect? On the contrary! In fact, I was far from it. But I started to think differently, and placed my focus on my present and future rather than on my past regrets and hurt.

Three publishers turned me down, but the fourth publisher loved my work, and my dream was born. Within the next three years, God placed me with an investor who believed in me, and six Christian Fiction novels came to life.

If I had not let go and let God work in my life, who knows where I would be today-- certainly not an author and motivational speaker, who has spoken in churches and Christian schools. That once-shy girl has no problem anymore speaking in front of hundreds. With God and confidence, anything is possible.

****

It is amazing how God works when we step back and actually allow Him to work. He will never open a door that He won't help you get through if you allow Him to.

****

For our light and momentary troubles are achieving for us an eternal glory that far outweighs them all. So we fix our eyes not on what is seen, but on what is unseen, for what is seen is temporary, but what is unseen is eternal. *(2 Corinthians 4:17-18) NIV*

****

When we realize that our troubles are only temporary, it makes it easier. The trouble is most of us can't hang on that long.

****

I sought the Lord, and He answered me; He delivered me from all my fears. *(Matthew34:4) NIV*

****

It saddens my heart when I hear of someone ending their life over a situation they felt they could no longer handle. Suicide is a permanent solution over a temporary situation. Only ***you*** hold the key to your own happiness.

Only ***you*** can make the decision to give your troubles to God and let Him handle them.

Maybe you are saying you just have no idea what I am going through and it isn't that simple. Maybe it's your marriage, or your special needs child. Maybe you're just exhausted from all you have to do in a day, and beyond stressed. Maybe you are facing a terminal illness or love someone who is. Maybe your finances are meager, and you have no idea how you will pay your mortgage this month.

I tell you; no matter what you are facing, ***nothing*** is too big for God.

What matters is how you handle the situation. Do you go into it kicking and screaming and lose your temper, or do you calmly assess the matter and face it head on in a calm manner?

Why do we hold on to the past?

We are like monkeys who just won't drop the banana.

Trappers who are catching monkeys for the zoo will take small cages to the jungle and place a bunch of bananas inside.

The monkey sees the tasty treat and reaches inside for the bananas, but no matter how hard it tries, it just can't pull the bunch through the rungs of the cage.

Even when it sees the trapper approaching and its heart is pounding, it will hang tight to the bananas and lever let them go, getting trapped because of its unwillingness to just turn loose and run.

Why are we like monkeys holding on to the bananas? Is it that sometimes we have grown so used to something that we don't want to let go? We get comfortable hanging on to it, and when we get comfortable, we stop growing in Christ.

When is the last time you held on to something and just wouldn't let it go? You gave it to Christ but then turned around and picked it right back up again. You keep picking it up because you have held on to it for so long it has become a part of you.

You've heard it said that God opens doors for you, but He also closes them for your benefit. When you know God has closed a door, you must stop opening it.

****

My husband was diagnosed with lymphatic cancer when he was twenty-seven years old, living in Miami, Florida down in Cutter Ridge.

The doctor told him, at best, he had three months to live; that it had progressed too far and there was nothing anyone could do. They asked him to allow them to do a case study on him until he died, because it was so bad at such a young age.

He hated leaving his young daughter, but he knew that no matter what happened he would be with Jesus, and peace came over him.

He left the doctor's office that day and went straight to the place he was employed at Arnold Packaging to tell his trusted friends--Rick Gibson, his boss and also a pastor, John Cahill, who was his friend and lead man.

They asked if they could lay hands on him and pray, and they prayed with such conviction Jim said it felt as if warm oil was running through his whole body. He felt God was preparing him to die and letting him know it would be okay.

Three days later, he returned to the doctor to start the study, only to find that there was no sign of cancer anywhere. Even though he had been exposed to benzene and acetone in vapor form and liquid for many hours a day, God had healed Jim's body completely.

That was in 1988.

I'm not sure why some are healed and some aren't, but I know for Jim he wasn't afraid when he got the diagnosis. He was ready for whatever God chose. He was able to let go and allow God to work in his life.

If you are facing things beyond your control, I encourage you to stay rooted in a Bible- believing church, around Christian friends. Get plugged in to the church. Don't just show up on Sundays, but volunteer to help out anywhere needed and become a server of God. And as with the last chapter--get a write-on, wipe-off marker and write on your mirror, **No problem is too big for God. I will not worry, but feel the peace of God. For with God, there isn't anything I cannot handle.**

Listen to Christian music and stay away from toxic friends. Read and watch things that are uplifting. Surround yourself with people who are leaders and are going somewhere. Stay positive and stay away from those who aren't.

You will find that if you live one day at a time and stop focusing on the problem but rather on your blessings, the sun will start to shine again.

Chapter Four

Forgiving Yourself of Past Wrongs

****

If we confess our sins, He is faithful and just to forgive us our sins and to cleanse us from all unrighteousness. *(! John 1:9) NIV*

****

Many people hold grudges against others, not letting go of past hurts, but not being able to forgive *yourself* is brutal.

When someone else is involved, there is always a way to work out your differences and forgive each other, but when it's you that you can't forgive, then the only way to true peace is with God.

****

It was March 31, 2015. I was excited because in just two weeks I was leaving for Miami, Florida, to climb aboard the Norwegian Epic and sail to Jamaica, Cozumel and the Grand Cayman Islands.

I had been working hard to lose weight and was excited at the size I had achieved. I was eager to dress up on the cruise ship and go out with my husband of one year and enjoy our belated honeymoon.

I'd never been on a cruise. Up until now, it had always been a dream of mine, and I wanted everything to be perfect.

My daughter Jennifer works in a high-dollar salon and also does makeup. I planned that night to go over and get her to show me the proper way to do my eyes. She had told me more than once I didn't do it right, and I was more than willing to learn so my seven- night cruise would be more than perfect, with me looking the best I possibly could.

It was warm that day. I remember I was wearing a pair of white shorts and a blue top. I was proud of myself because it was the first time I had fit into those shorts in years. (And yes, I had saved them because they were my favorites.)

I drove a white Jeep Liberty, but for some reason my husband's Silverado pickup truck was sitting behind mine, and instead of moving it, I asked Jim for his key, telling him I would be back as soon as I could.

I still remember the drive over--just a short five-minute drive as we only live a few miles apart. I was thinking about my upcoming vacation and thanking God for His blessings. I was so incredibly happy in my life that there were times I had to remind myself how far I had come since my days of depression.

My son was now thirteen and in the eighth grade. He had gone back to public school and was thriving and had friends.

After three years of being single after my divorce, Jim had been good for both of us.

Life was great, with no complaints. I was on top of the world, living at the lake with a great marriage, good job, author of six published books and a motivational speaker. My life had certainly changed over the past four years, and I was eternally grateful.

I learned something that day; that no matter how great life seems to be, everything can change in a moment.

As I entered my daughter's apartment complex, I noticed many children playing on both sides of the street and to my left in the playground. There are many speed bumps there, so I was going very slowly.

Jim's truck sits very high off the ground and I hate driving it. I'm still not sure what made me take it that day. As I was going over another speed bump, I observed a young boy to my right riding on a scooter. He looked directly at me and smiled and I saw him stop. There were adults there also, holding on to hands of little ones.

As I looked back to my left, I felt another speed bump, and then I heard everyone scream. Horror filled me, knowing there wasn't another speed bump there. What had I run over going so slowly?

I stopped the truck and got out trying to see what all the commotion was about, and all the while my heart was racing. Had I hit an animal I had not seen?

There are no words to describe what happened next. It was as if time stood still as everything went in slow motion. There on the ground just behind the truck was the small boy that I had saw with the green scooter.

Everyone was rushing to the small boy who now lay motionless on the ground.

"Oh Jesus," I screamed. "Please help him!"

How could I have run over him when I was sure I saw him look directly at me and stop, knowing I was there? How could this be happening, when I had been so careful observing my surroundings?

I heard someone say that 911 had been called and another say he had stopped breathing. I yelled out we need to do CPR, but a lady gently took hold of my arm, told me she was a nurse and that we couldn't because the tire had run over his chest, and to wait on the ambulance.

I cried out for Jesus to help us and not let him die. I begged everyone around to help me pray.

It seemed almost everyone there only spoke Spanish, and I wasn't sure if they understood me as I cried out to God.

Within minutes, the police came on the scene as well as the ambulance. I was still running around begging them to do something. I am certain I have never been more afraid in my life; not that I was in trouble, but that this young boy was going to lose his life, and there was nothing any of us could do.

A woman came to me who spoke a little English and told me that she had seen what happened and assured me it wasn't my fault. She said he had a habit of playing chicken with the cars and had been warned many times to stop playing in the road.

Maybe she thought that knowing this would give me some comfort, yet still, I couldn't wrap my mind around what had happened.

By now, several people were coming up to me and assuring me it wasn't my fault, yet still I cried. What did it really matter whose fault it was? Here he lay, so still, as the paramedics worked on him. I heard one of the paramedics say we have a heartbeat.

"Thank You, Jesus," I screamed out loud.

A deputy walked over to me and asked if I was the one who had hit him. I nodded my head and continued to cry. "Will he be okay?" I asked.

"We sure hope so. Can I see your license, please?" he asked. He seemed kind and sympathetic. I could tell he hated what had happened as much as I did.

I was shaking as I made my way toward the truck for my purse. Horror filled me as I realized I had not gotten my purse out of my car when I had left the house.

I tried to explain to him that I had gotten in my husband's truck to come visit my daughter and had forgotten to grab my purse, but that we just lived a couple of miles down the road. He shook his head and told me to please call my husband to bring it to me.

Thank God I had remembered to bring my phone with me.

I can't remember exactly what I told Jim when he answered, but he and my sons were there very quickly.

By the time they arrived, the law already had the area roped off with the truck and I in the center and had already placed the young boy in the ambulance and were leaving with him.

Jim ran to me and hugged me tightly. I just kept crying, telling him what had happened. When the police officer asked me to fill out a statement, I was shaking too badly to write, and he told Jim that he could write it for me.

My daughter and granddaughter had heard the commotion and had come out of their apartment. The officer told her to stay back, but she told him she was my daughter and crossed under the tape anyway. He allowed her to come to me.

She was crying, too, and told me she knew the boy I had hit because just two hours before that he had run out in front of her car, and she had told him to please get out of the road before someone hit him. She took my shaking hands and prayed with me.

The officer came to us again and asked if he could please search the truck and my purse. He said everyone says that the little boy ran out in front of you, but it is still required for us to search.

We stood back and told him to go ahead. Jim told me they were looking for any alcohol or drugs that might have impaired me and my thinking.

After they had searched the truck and found nothing, he came to me again and told me that they were waiting on a special investigator to come and take pictures so we would all have to wait a bit longer before we could leave.

Darkness was now setting in, and many people had gone back inside. I told my daughter to take my granddaughter back inside where it was warm.

My son wrapped a coat around me as I shivered, but I am certain I wasn't just shivering from the now-cold air. It was just so surreal to me, that I had run over a five-year-old boy, and his life was hanging in the balance.

After the investigator was finished, the officer came to me again. "I hate to tell you this, but I need you to go with me to the hospital and take a Blood Alcohol Test. We didn't find anything, and I can tell you aren't impaired, but this is necessary and will also cover you should they try to prosecute you."

My head was now spinning. Could I be in trouble for something that was an accident?

Oh, how his parents must feel! I wondered if it was his parents I had seen holding his hand or just people from the apartments; so much was now going through my mind.

I asked him if Jim and I could follow him to the hospital and he said, "No ma'am, you will have to ride with me."

I had never been in the back of a patrol car before. With a heavy heart, I held out my hands for him to place handcuffs on me.

He smiled and said, "That won't be necessary."

The ride over seemed to take forever, even though it was just five miles down the road. I talked to him all the way, telling him I appreciated how kind he was and to please continue to pray for the little boy. He was not allowed to tell me the boy's name, but it didn't matter because I told him God knew his name.

I told the people at the hospital to please pray for him also. And later that night when I arrived home, at almost midnight, I told all my Facebook fans from my author site to please pray as well.

I went to bed broken. Even though I knew it wasn't my fault, that he was playing a silly game trying to beat my truck, he had lost. And because of the chain of events that led me to my daughter's that day, I was the one he went out in front of. It was the truck I was driving that ran over his small body.

The next day, that same officer knocked on my door, and as I opened the door, he removed his hat. I almost fell to the floor. I knew in my heart he had bad news, but I couldn't bear to hear it.

"Is he going to be okay?" I asked.

With tears in his eyes he answered, "No ma'am. I am sorry; he passed away forty minutes after you hit him yesterday, but I couldn't tell you until his next-of-kin was notified. Plus your faith was so strong I couldn't bear to tell you."

Jim wrapped his arms around me as I cried out. "I killed someone, Jim. A little boy is dead because I killed him!"

"You didn't kill him, Karen," Jim said to me. "It wasn't your fault."

But it didn't matter that it wasn't my fault; he was still dead, and he was never coming back again all because I decided to go to my daughter's to learn how to do my eye makeup, of all things. Something so unimportant led me there, and now he was gone.

For days and weeks and even months, I could see a child who looked like him and would fall to pieces. I could accidentally run over a squirrel or a rabbit and sob like a baby. How was I ever going to be able to forgive myself and move on with my life?

Jim set up an appointment for me to counsel with someone, and even though it made me feel somewhat better, the pain was still there. I felt guilty when I laughed and would remind myself I didn't deserve to laugh.

I held all that pain inside and stopped reminding my family or my husband. Instead, I would cry when I was alone and question God. Why me? What could possibly come out of this that was good?

It wasn't until I was doing year one of **Kineo,** *(to move forward)* a theology class my husband and I were taking, that I was taught to journal with God.

God showed me through journaling and hearing His voice that the little boy was okay and with Him. That this earth could never compare to where he was now with Jesus, and that I had to let it go and move on, so I could fulfill my purpose and allow God to work through me.

Through the Spirit I was able to see him and tell him I was sorry. I saw that he was happy and with Jesus, and I was once again able to go on with my life.

Sure, there are times I shudder when Satan brings it all back to me, but my God is bigger than Satan, and I remind him of that each time he plays tricks with my mind. Satan can't get to any of us as long as we don't allow him to. When we are in Jesus and Jesus is in us, Satan has no power over us.

Some of you may think I'm crazy, and that too is okay, for if you do, then you just don't know Jesus the way I do. And I'm so glad you are now reading this book; it is certainly for you. (I smile as I write this, knowing how true it is).

Now you may be saying, oh sure, you didn't intentionally mean to do it, why would you need to forgive yourself? Or what about those who have intentionally sinned, and because of it think Jesus would never forgive them?

There are so many things that can be done intentionally. Maybe you were even saved already but are just not living close to God, or are not yet ready to really form a relationship with Him.

I have run into all kinds of people who have opened up and shared parts of their life with me. Things like infidelity, adultery, abortion, homosexuality, theft, drugs, alcohol, prostitution, murder, molestation, pornography, deception, domestic violence, and the list goes on and on.

Or maybe you can't forgive yourself of something simple; something you said that you wished you hadn't, or something you should have done and didn't. In any case, there are all types of reasons one may hold a grudge against themselves.

If this is you, it's time to release it and let it go. If it is something you are still currently doing, then I suggest you take it before God and seek Christian counseling.

It isn't easy coming to terms with the things you did wrong. Satan loves reminding you of the regrets of your past, telling you that you are worthless, and making you feel that there is no way out of that thing you did wrong.

Jesus came to forgive us of our sins by taking those sins upon Himself at the cross. When He said "It is finished," it was just that.

When we confess our sins to Him, He forgives us. He doesn't need us reminding Him daily, because when He truly forgives us, He forgets it. You see, Jesus doesn't hold grudges like we do.

When the Bible tells us that we must forgive in order to be forgiven, that doesn't just mean that we have to forgive others. That same verse applies to ourselves also. We are just as important to God as anyone else.

Get out with nature and really talk to God. Present Him with the bare facts (even though He already knows it all) and take it before Him. Talk to Him as you would your best friend (because He is) and tell Him you are ready to put it behind you. Ask Him to help you forgive yourself, and then place it before Him.

****

Once, I had issues of deliberate sins that I kept beating myself up over. It took me six years to forgive myself of doing things I knew were wrong. I knew God had forgiven me, but I just couldn't forgive myself, and by hating myself for things I wish I hadn't done, I was holding a grudge against someone God loved (Me).

I wrote everything down on paper, and I sealed it up in an envelope, and I placed it in an imaginary monkey cage and let it go.

You might even go to the top of a mountain and rip the paper to shreds and let the wind send the pieces cascading down. Or maybe a bridge or dam and toss the pieces over the side. No matter how you decide to do it, get rid of it and forgive yourself. You cannot go back and change the past, but you can change the present, which changes the future.

Chapter Five

Forgiving Others

****

Be Kind and compassionate to one another, forgiving each other, just as Christ forgave you. *(Ephesians 4:32 NIV)*

****

For some, forgiving others is even harder than forgiving themselves. In fact, many have held grudges for years and purposely avoid the person they hold the grudge against.

What if the person you can't forgive isn't even here anymore? Maybe something happened between the two of you many years ago, and they have long since passed, but the bitterness inside your heart hasn't.

God hates when we hold grudges. In fact, His word is filled with verses that clearly tell us if we cannot forgive others, then we cannot be forgiven ourselves.

****

And when you stand praying, if you hold anything against anyone, forgive him, so that your Father in heaven may forgive your sins. *(Mark 11:25)*

****

Think about it--if we ask God to forgive us and fully expect that He will, isn't that being a bit selfish when we can't forgive another?

Why would you ask Him to do something you aren't willing to do yourself? That's the same as being a hypocrite.

When we harbor hurt feelings and bitterness, it only hurts us. We become a prisoner of our own pain and suffering, until it gets so bad it festers like a sore. It becomes a way of life for us, and we sit around in our own pity party and sulk and pout.

When we sulk and pout and constantly think about that thing we can't let go of, we lose our joy, and without joy life is meaningless. We become unproductive, and an unproductive person is useless to God.

There are many kinds of unforgiveness. But one of the most common, other than not being able to forgive yourself, is holding a grudge against your parents, siblings or family members.

Let's face it, not everyone is blessed with great parents. And sometimes they really are great, but we get to the age that we think we know everything and they don't, and sometimes we go our own way when, in fact, we should have listened.

Molestation is another hurt some hold all of their lives. Maybe your father, sibling, family member or neighbor molested you as a child, and you've gone through your entire life filled with bitterness.

No matter what you are having trouble forgiving, just know that God is enough! He is enough to get you through all your struggles and storms, and if you allow Him, He will mend the broken pieces and put you together whole. But there isn't anything He can do if you shut Him out and continue to hold on to your pain.

****

For if you forgive others their trespasses, your heavenly Father will also forgive you, but if you do not forgive others their trespasses, neither will your Father forgive your trespasses. (Matthew 6:14-15)

****

That's a powerful verse if you think about it. Imagine someday standing before God, and He withholds some of your eternal blessings because of the bitterness you had in your heart.

"But I asked for forgiveness of that," you remind Him. He smiles down at you and reminds you that you wouldn't understand forgiveness, since you were not able to forgive others yourself.

****

I was given permission from a friend to share with you her story.

For thirty-seven years, she held bitterness and anger toward the young man who ran his car into her daughter and son-in-law's car one evening and not only killed himself but her daughter as well.

It was her only child, and even after thirty-seven years, it still devastated her each time she thought about that dreadful day. There wasn't a day that went by that she didn't long to have her daughter alive, just to talk to her about life.

She was eighty-three years old when she picked up my sixth book, ***Amazing Grace, The Ultimate Forgiveness***, and was finally able to turn loose of the hurt and pain she had carried for so many years.

It had been a pain that sometimes consumed her with anger—anger over the fact that the young man had been drinking.

I saw her the morning she finished the book and found her crying. She said she had cried often the previous night and couldn't put the book down. She felt that she was meant to read the book, and God had shown her it was time to let the pain go and forgive him in her heart.

The accident had happened in a very small northern town in Georgia, so the young man and her daughter had been buried in the same cemetery.

One day, she and I were placing new flowers on her daughter's grave when I asked whose grave was so far from the others at the edge of the woods. It was all grown over with weeds, and there were no flowers to speak of.

She told me that is where the young man's family had laid him to rest.

I walked over and looked at the grave and calculated the age he was when he died. He was only twenty-one years old, and I am sure he didn't set out that day to harm anyone or end his life. He made a mistake, and it cost him everything.

I leaned down and pulled many of the weeds from the grave and walked back to her. The flowers we were taking away from her daughter's grave still looked good, as she changed the artificial flowers out often.

"Did you really forgive him?" I asked.

She smiled. "I did. I am no longer upset with him. Your book helped me with that and showed me what I should have done many years ago."

"Can I take these and place them on his grave?" I asked, holding the flowers we were replacing.

"Sure, that would be good; he needs some flowers."

When we left the cemetery that day, there was a peace about her I had never seen before. I knew that in her heart she truly had forgiven him.

All those years, it hadn't hurt him at all that she couldn't forgive him; it had only hurt her and caused her pain and grief and anguish. For thirty-seven years, she had been a prisoner locked away, finding no real joy in life because of that bitterness.

When we choose to give our pain to God and forgive, then and only then can we move on. Only then can we find the joy and happiness that God has for us. Only then can we be forgiven ourselves.

So if you are holding anything against someone, it's time to let it go. You must forgive them even if they don't ask. If it is a situation where you also did or said things you shouldn't have, maybe they are holding a grudge against you, too. Why not start by being the first to say you're sorry? Someone has to make the first move, and it's okay to be the bigger person. And remember, even if they don't tell you that they are sorry or act like they forgive you, forgive them anyway.

If someone from your past hurt you and they have passed away, go to the cemetery if you have to, and talk to them. Sometimes it's good to get it out in the open, and just hear yourself say it out loud.

Pride is a sin, and we let pride keep us from making the first step, always waiting on someone else. It's amazing how good it feels when you come face-to-face with that thing that bothers you, and you are finally able to cast it aside.

You may be saying that I have no idea what I am talking about because I haven't walked in your shoes and I don't know the circumstance and I can't imagine your pain, but trust me, I do.

Remember, God is enough! He loves it when we move past our comfort zone and make amends. He needs you empty so He can fill you with His presence. He can't use you if there is anything still inside that prevents you from fully relying on Him.

Don't put off tomorrow what needs to be taken care of today. Pick up the phone, write the letter, drive to the cemetery, but do it today, so when you leave this world you can face God knowing you have forgiven and have a clear heart.

*****

I suggest you read my sixth book, ***Amazing Grace, The Ultimate Forgiveness.***

www.sbpra.com/KarenAyers

Chapter Six

It Matters Where You Go To Church

****

My wonderful pastor at Christ Fellowship Church in Dawsonville, Georgia once said it matters where you go to church. At first I thought that was a pretty terrible thing to say because it was as if he were putting down other churches, until I listened to the whole sermon and I realized it really ***does*** matter where you go to church.

When I was growing up, my parents were gospel singers. They traveled all over to various churches and sang with a band.

When they were home, we went to a small Baptist church every time the door opened. We never missed a Wednesday night service or Sunday morning service unless they were booked someplace else. I was the kid always at Vacation Bible School, and many times I went to several different ones, not just our own church.

With that being said, you can see why I know how different churches worship. There are so many denominations that preach and teach and worship differently.

Baptist, Methodist, Pentecostal, Episcopalian, Catholic, Holiness, Eastern Orthodox, Presbyterian, Non-Denominational, Jehovah's Witness, Lutheran, Church of Nazarene, Seventh-Day Adventist, Church of Christ, and many more.

What I am about to say may offend you, but listen with your head and not your emotions.

As I said before, I was raised in a Baptist church. I'm not putting down the Baptists, so don't twist my words. In fact, I know many wonderful God-fearing people who are Baptist, but let me explain before you lay this book down and say that's it.

My parents were wonderful people who raised me in church and told me all about Jesus. Each week I sat in the pews of so many churches and listened to the pastor preach on hellfire and where we would all end up if we weren't saved.

In all the years of listening to my parents and the pastors of many of the churches including my own, never did I hear once that Jesus is, in fact, God in the flesh.

Never did I hear that after we are saved it is the Holy Spirit who comes and dwells inside of us, and not Jesus in our heart, as I was taught.

Never did anyone tell me that Jesus is in all sixty-six books in the Bible, from Genesis to Revelation, and that He always has been since the beginning of time, even before he was born of a virgin.

****

In Genesis, He is the Breath of Life.

In Exodus, He is the Passover Lamb.

In Leviticus, He is our High Priest.

In Numbers, He is a pillar of cloud by day and a pillar of fire by night.

In Deuteronomy, He is the Prophet like unto Moses.

In Joshua, He is the Captain of our Salvation.

In Judges, He is our Judge and Lawgiver.

In Ruth, He is our Kinsman Redeemer.

In First and Second Samuel, He is our Trusted Prophet.
In Kings and Chronicles, He is our Reigning King.
In Ezra and Nehemiah, He is the re-builder of broken down walls of human life.
In Esther, He is Mordecai.
In Job, He is our Ever-Living Redeemer.
In Psalm, He is our Shepherd.
In Proverbs and Ecclesiastes, He is our Wisdom.
In the Song of Solomon, He is the Loving Bridegroom.
In Isaiah, He is the Prince of Peace.
In Jeremiah, He is the Righteous Branch.
In Lamentations, He is the Weeping Prophet.
In Ezekiel, He's the Son of Man.
In Daniel, He's the fourth man in life's fiery furnace.
In Hosea, He's the Faithful Husband.
In Joel, He is the Baptizer of the Holy Ghost and fire.
In Amos, He is a Burden Bearer.
In Obadiah, He is Mighty to Save.
In Jonah, He is the Forgiving God.
In Micah, He is the Messenger of beautiful feet.
In Nahum, He is our Strength and Shield.
In Habakkuk, He is the Great Evangelist crying for revival.
In Zephaniah, He is our Savior.
In Haggai, He is the Restorer of God's lost heritage.
In Zechariah, He is the Fountain.
In Malachi, He is the Star of Righteousness.
In Matthew, He is Messiah.
In Mark, He is The Miracle Worker.
In Luke, He is The Son of Man.
In John, He is Son of God.
In Acts, He is Ascended Lord.
In Romans, He is the Justifier.

In First and Second Corinthians, He is the last Adam.

In Galatians, He is the One who sets us free.

In Ephesians, He is Christ of Riches.

In Philippians, He is God who meets our every need.

In Colossians, He is Fullness of the Godhead.

In First and Second Thessalonians, He is the soon-coming King.

In First and Second Timothy, He is Mediator between God and man.

In Titus, He is Blessed Hope.

In Philemon, He is a Friend closer than a brother.

In Hebrews, He is Blood that washes away our sins.

In James, He is the Great Physician.

In First and Second Peter, He is the Chief Shepherd.

In First, Second and Third John, He is Everlasting Love.

In Jude, He is God our Savior.

In Revelation, He is the King of Kings and Lord of Lords.

****

Did you *know* this?

Are you thinking, "Wow," just as I did when it finally hit me that in all the years of "*church*," I had not truly been taught the true Word of God? So much had been left out and skipped over.

So much was pushed aside because it was too uncomfortable to speak aloud, watered down and sugar-coated.

Sure, I had been taught the only way to the Father was through the Son and that I must believe in Jesus and be born again, but no one told me what to do after that.

Never had I learned about the gifts of the Spirit.

Never did anyone tell me that the Holy Spirit is the one I pray to because Jesus is on the right hand of the Father in Heaven, waiting to come back to take His bride. (And by the way, in case you were never told this, His bride is all of us who believe and have been saved.)

Can Jesus and God hear me? Of course they can, but it is the Holy Spirit who dwells inside of us. It is the Holy Spirit who whispers in our ear and guides us and warns us of things to come if we only listen.

The Trinity is all three separate, yet the same. Amazing, isn't it?

So now you can understand how very important it is to plant yourself in a church that teaches the true word of the Holy Bible, God's Holy Word.

God doesn't just want you to get saved and go on about your life. He has so much more planned for you than you could ever imagine. I will get into that soon.

I'm sure, if you are reading this, you are thinking about ***your*** church, the church ***you*** attend regularly. In your mind, you are thinking about some of the past sermons and summing it all up. If you are in a church that has taught you all the things I just mentioned, then you found yourself a good one, but if not........

You see, God intended for you to assemble yourself with other believers to worship and to learn. Church isn't just a place you go each week and talk about the women's committee, bingo night, or the picnic planned for the following weekend.

It doesn't matter that it is where your parents went and their parents before them; if they are not teaching you the whole word, then you are wasting your time.

I've known people in their eighties who have told me they don't understand most of the Bible, and it saddens me. It saddens me because they lived their life going to watered-down churches that are afraid to preach the Word the way God has written it. The way God intended it to be read.

Have you ever wondered why God breathed the words in the Bible to so many men? If He thought all the words were important enough to be written down, then He had a reason for doing so. His desire was for His children to read it in its entirety, beginning to end, leaving no stone unturned.

Do you ever wonder what comes next after salvation? The day of our salvation is the first day of eternity. Jesus paid a high price for you, and He expects you to do more than sit on the sidelines and wait to die to be with Him. He wants to be with you now--today. This is why He sent the Holy Spirit to dwell inside of you so that you would never be alone.

I could go on and on about the things God wants for you, but I will wait and share that a bit later. As for now, I need you to understand that in order to be the very best you can be, you must fully understand God's word, and you can't learn God's word without going to a church that teaches it in its fullness.

Maybe you're thinking that will never work, because your denomination doesn't teach about the gifts of the Spirit, or speaking in tongues. All I can say to that is don't be afraid to change your denomination. It isn't a denomination that gets you to heaven anyway; it's whether you have a relationship with Jesus or not.

****

Call to Me and I will answer you and tell you great and unsearchable things you do not know. *(Jeremiah 33:3)*

****

It's true you don't have to go to church to go to heaven, but the fact is, if we really desire a relationship with Jesus, one that you can grow in and get closer to Him, it is almost impossible to get there without attending church on a weekly basis.

Assembling yourself around other Christian believers just does something to you. And when you are attending a church that is bold enough to speak the truth and not care whose toes they step on, then you will learn and grow in Christ.

There's nothing I hate worse than attending a ***dead church***, and when I say dead, I mean there is absolutely no spirit there. A dead church worries more about the number of people they have in the seats than the number of people who were saved.

A dead church feels cold and rushed, leaving out so much of the Bible that was important enough to God that He inspired His believers to write it down so it could be shared with us.

You see, when you stop growing, you begin to rot. And I don't mean growing taller, but growing spiritually. God cannot use an unwilling vessel, and it's hard to be willing when you haven't a clue how to be.

There is no shame in leaving one church and moving to another. But, whatever you do, don't church-hop. So many hop from church to church and never settle. They are forever finding reasons to move on; usually because of something the pastor said they didn't agree with, or they found out someone in the congregation wasn't perfect, as they assumed Christians were.

Where it has been said, "***If that's a Christian, I don't want any part of it***," then whoever said it is going to church for the wrong reason. Remember, you are there to worship God, not man. No man is perfect, not even the pastor.

Remember, hypocrites are everywhere, so you can either go to church with them or die and go to hell with them; just don't let them stop you from having a relationship with Jesus.

When it comes to your relationship with Jesus, only you can go after that.

Only you can plant yourself in a church where you can grow and learn.

Only you will stand before God someday; no one will be standing with you.

Only you can store up your treasures in heaven; no one else can do that for you.

So ask yourself this question: is where I'm attending church feeding my spirit?

Don't think about all the friends you have there or how many generations before you went there. Don't think about the position you hold or how much you are counted on. Don't think about the upcoming picnic or how disappointed Mrs. Jones would be if you left.

Is your spirit being fed each week? If the answer is no, take it before God and pray about it. I mean earnestly pray about it and ask God what He has for you. Follow His guidance and go where He leads you. I can assure you, He will never lead you astray.

Chapter Seven

Serving God as You Serve Others

****

Be wise in the way you act toward outsiders; make the most of every opportunity. Let your conversation be always full of grace, seasoned with salt, so that you may know how to answer everyone. *(Colossians 4:5-6)NIV*

****

God loves a willing vessel. While it is true that it is not by our works we are saved, when we think about what Jesus did for us when He died on that cross, why wouldn't we want to live every day serving Him?

Each day my prayer is for the Holy Spirit to send me where I need to go, show me what I need to see, and tell me what I need to hear or say.

I promise if you start praying that prayer and be willing to do as He guides you to do, He will use you in a mighty way.

I must admit, it wasn't always easy to do what God was putting on my heart; in fact, there were times I balked against Him and refused, thinking how silly I would look or what other people would think.

It takes courage to talk to a stranger about God or lay hands on them and pray. I have learned through experience that the more you step out of your comfort zone and be a willing vessel for God, the easier it becomes.

The more you are willing, the harder the tasks become, but the fear you once knew diminishes and is replaced by courage you never knew.

When God knows He can trust you to do minor things, He will trust you with major things.

There is just no better feeling in the world than leading someone to Christ and praying the prayer of salvation with them, to see the joy on their face as they realize for the first time in their life they now understand what true joy is.

****

For even the Son of man did not come to be served, but to serve, and to give His life as a ransom for many. *(Mark 10:45)*

****

I'm not only an author and motivational speaker, I am also a CNA; some people like to call me a caregiver of geriatric patients. While my dream is to travel the world and lead others to Christ, my reality has been taking care of the elderly.

I love what I do and enjoy helping wherever needed. I have worked as many as one hundred twenty hours in one week. Some ask, how do you do it? I smile and say, God holds me up. It's what He urges me to do, so how can I complain?

I was once a caregiver of a hospice patient. We became extremely close the last two and a half months of her life. She had lived the majority of her life as a priest's wife and knew God and the Bible well.

I was not sure what God's plan was for my being there other than to earn extra income, so I questioned Him. "Am I here for something other than help with my finances or lending her a helping hand?"

On the third night with her, the Holy Spirit spoke to me and showed me what He needed of me and why I was there.

I asked her if I could pray with her before she went to bed, and she happily said, "Of course!"

I got down on my knees and placed my hands in hers and proceeded to pray aloud. I thanked God for our blessings and our children and grandchildren. I thanked Him for bringing her into my life and prayed for her peace over the situation she was going through. When I was finished, she said a very short five-word prayer and we both said amen.

After a couple of weeks, she asked me why I thought God still had her here and how long she was going to have to suffer?

I told her as boldly but gently as I could that He wanted her to pour out her heart to Him, and that He showed me that in the Spirit. He wanted to know her thoughts, and for her to love on Him as He loved on her.

She looked at me a bit confused and said, "He already knows my thoughts before I speak them; why do I need to say them out loud?"

I gently took her hand and told her I know my youngest son also. I know he is fifteen and his favorite food is spaghetti. I know the way he loves to dress and his favorite color is yellow like mine. I probably know more about him than anyone because he is my son, but if all he ever did each and every day was come in and say, "Hey Mom," and never spent time talking to me, I would be extremely sad and hunger for his time and attention.

She admitted that she never thought of it in that way.

In the weeks that followed, I saw the way she prayed each night before bedtime change drastically. In fact, her prayers, which in the past were just a few words became ten-minute prayers where she poured her heart out to God. She called all her children and their children by name and prayed for each of them. She thanked God for her blessings and her life.

As I said before, it takes courage to share with someone what the Holy Spirit desires for you to share, but the reward afterwards is priceless--just seeing her pour out her heart to God, and knowing it was His desire to have that close relationship with His daughter, a daughter who was coming to the end of her earthly life.

I was proud that I could be the willing vessel that the Holy Spirit could use to carry her even closer to Him than ever before.

Now what if I had not shared with her the things the Holy Spirit was leading me to share? What if she had passed away and never really learned to pour out her heart to Him? Would she have still gone to heaven? Of course, she would have; she knew Jesus to be her savior, but that closeness with Him that He desired made the crossing over better and gave her peace.

****

What does it profit, my brother, if someone says he has faith but does not have works? Can faith save him? If a brother or sister is naked and destitute of daily food, and one of you says to them, "Depart in peace, be warmed and filled," but you do not give them the things which are needed for the body, what does it profit? Thus also faith by itself, if it does not have works, is dead.

But someone will say, "You have faith, and I have works." Show me your faith without your works, and I will show you my

faith by my works. You believe that there is one God. You do well. Even the demons believe and tremble! But do you want to know, O foolish man, that faith without works is dead? Was not Abraham our father justified by works when he offered Isaac his son on the altar?

Do you see that faith was working together with his works, and by works faith was made perfect? And the scripture was fulfilled which says, "Abraham believed God, and it was accounted to him for righteousness. And he was called the friend of God. You see then that a man is justified by works, and not by faith only. *(James 2:14-26) NKJV*

****

If, after we are saved, we do nothing but go about our lives and never let our light so shine for Him, it's like a child you give a gift to. You worked hard so the child could have the gift of a lifetime. It cost you much to be able to give it to them, and it brought you such joy when they opened it and you saw the happiness on their face.

But after a couple of days, the excitement of the gift that had cost you so much dwindled and they put it down, never to pick it up again.

The gift was still theirs and there if they ever wanted to pick it back up. You would never take it back; after all, it was theirs to keep. But day after day there were just too many distractions, and it became a gift that wasn't important anymore. And you couldn't help but wonder if they ever really appreciated it at all?

Jesus suffered and died the most horrifying death one could imagine. He was stripped naked and beaten and bruised and nailed to a cross and hung up in clear view to be laughed at and mocked as he died.

He did this for **you** and for **me.** It was His gift for all of us, and it cost Him everything. He was sinless and yet took all of our sins upon himself, so that we could be forgiven and live forever with Him in eternity.

Your salvation and what He did for you will by far be the best gift you will ever receive. No amount of money or fame could ever take the place of your hereafter.

When we serve others, we are giving back to God what He gave to us. We are showing our love and gratitude for what He did for us.

By sharing the ***good news*** of Jesus and obeying the Spirit, we allow others to experience His love through our kindness.

My Theology teacher once told me that Jesus just oozes out of me. That was probably the best compliment I have ever gotten, and I have never forgotten it, nor will I ever.

I pray daily that God take away the thoughts in my mind that crowd up unnecessary space and replace them with Him. I lived much too long doing things that weren't pleasing to Him, and never again do I want to waste my days not taking every opportunity to do as He desires.

Ask yourself again, if you were to be on trial for being a Christian, would there be enough evidence to convict you?

If your daily routine for the past year were to be displayed before a jury of twelve, would they undoubtedly say you were a Christian, or would they have to spend hours going over evidence, scratching their heads and just not able to come up with enough to prove you guilty?

****

Your attitude should be the same as that of Christ Jesus. *(Philippians 2:5)NIV*

****

How do others see you?

Do you hold your head high and smile at those you meet?

Do you stop whenever needed to give a helping hand?

Do you ever tell someone how much Jesus loves them?

Are you someone others love to be around, or do you constantly cause trouble and strife and drama wherever you go?

Are you someone who leads people toward Christ or away from Christ--as in partying or hanging out in bars, doing drugs or smoking pot?

Do you earn what you have or do you manipulate to get what you want?

Do you comfort those around you, or do you use language displeasing to God to look tough before others?

Are you a leader or a follower?

Would you desire your children to grow up to be just like you? Or do you pray they take a different path?

Do you compliment others or laugh and make fun of those less fortunate.

Do you hand the man holding the sign on the street money if God places it on your heart, or say no, Lord, I worked hard for my money and he will just spend it on beer?

When you see a cashier at the store who looks as if they are having a bad day, do you storm off rudely, or do you smile and gently make conversation, showing Jesus' love for them?

If your pastor followed you all week, would you change your routine, or would you feel confident he would be pleased?

Do you act the same on Friday and Saturday nights as you do on Sunday mornings?

Do you attend church to worship and learn more of God's word, or do you stay home and say you don't need church to go to heaven?

Are the people you hang out with ones that you hope your children learn from and look up to, or do you meet your friends in secret hoping your family doesn't know?

God wants your best and deserves your best.

****

So because you are lukewarm—neither cold nor hot, I am about to spit you from My mouth. *(Revelation 3:16) NIV*

****

Jesus dislikes a lukewarm Christian. How do you know if you are a lukewarm Christian? Ask yourself these questions.

1. Do you only pray when you have a problem?
2. Are you always asking God for things instead of thanking Him?
3. Do you twist scripture to justify sin?
4. Do you think just because you go to church you can live like hell the rest of the week?
5. Do you compromise with God's Word?
6. Do you really only desire to be a Christian to keep you from hell?
7. You are never truly sorry for your sins or really desire to change.
8. Do you compare yourself to others?

9. You very rarely share your faith with others.
10. You care more about what others think than what God thinks.
11. You have no desire to get closer to Christ.
12. You are never willing to make sacrifices.
13. You are constantly saying, "Do not judge."

****

You cannot be a part-time Christian and live full-time for God. And to truly live full-time for God, you must be willing to serve others daily and allow the Holy Spirit to work through you to fulfill His purpose. There must be no doubt in anyone's mind that you are, in fact, a Christian and ooze Jesus from every pore.

Maybe you are asking yourself, how can I do that? How can I spend my entire day working for God? I am too busy. Maybe you think God wants you to be happy because He loves you so much, and that you couldn't possibly be happy if you invested every moment in Him.

Maybe you go days and weeks without actually talking to Him, because you never really think about Him until you are in a crisis and then call on Him for help.

You see, when you make the decision that you are going to live for God and truly mean it, it becomes a way of life for you. You don't have to get up looking for people to serve; they just come your way. God will place them directly in your path, because He wants to bless them, and He knows He can bless them through you.

Without us--a body, the Holy Spirit cannot bless others. He uses us to bless others and others to bless us.

I want to share with you something my pastor preached on one day that really made me stop and think.

There are 7.4 billion people in this world. 300,000 new people are born each and every day! Isn't that amazing?

And just think, 2.3 million people claim to be Christians and know Jesus Christ and that He died for their sins. That's 31% of the world's population, which means 69% of the world's population are not Christians, meaning 5.1 billion have never accepted Jesus as their savior.

42% of the world is known as an unreachable people group; that's over 3.1 million people! These are people without a church movement. People with no Christian influence who have never heard the message of Jesus, and many have no way of hearing the gospel.

Out of the 55,300,000 people who die each year in the world, 17,143,000 people will go to heaven because they are in a blood covenant with Jesus and have been saved, leaving 69% that are unsaved. This means 38,157,000 people will die and go to hell because they have never been saved.

23 million people have never heard the name of Jesus.

151,500 people die every day. 46,986 have been saved and 104,539 have not been saved.

64,000 people stepped out into eternity today and have never heard the gospel!!

Don't you think it's sad that people will die and go to hell because they have never had anyone like you to make them feel loved or special and share the good news that Jesus loved them and died for them, so they can be forgiven and have eternal life?

Have you ever heard it said that people don't care how much you know until they know how much you care? Or how about, it is more blessed to give than to receive?

Why do you think missionaries feed the hungry ***before*** they try to teach them about God?

Because people naturally just listen to someone who treats them well and is kind to them.

We are to be a living sacrifice for God, to live our life pleasing to Him, and to help all those we come in contact with who need it. And we must assume that all we meet do, because honestly we all need to know about the love of Jesus and what He did for us.

Now I'm not saying spend every waking moment telling everyone you meet about Jesus, but I am saying make the most of every waking moment, always being humble and kind, and if the Holy Spirit leads you to tell them more, you will be someone they will want to listen to.

Chapter Eight

Hearing God's Voice

****

Before we can ever hear our favorite radio station, we have to be within its range and be tuned in to that particular station; otherwise, there is no way we can hear the station clear enough for it to be intelligible. This is also true when hearing God's voice, which is the Holy Spirit within us.

Lost people are not a part of the body of Christ, because they have never been unified with Him. Therefore, they cannot hear His voice except to be called to repent and come to Him.

Most Christians remember what it was like when the Holy Spirit called to you. Maybe you were in a powerful church service. Maybe you were reading a book or listening to a song on the radio that really hit a nerve and shook you up a bit.

In any case, that tug on your heart was Him calling to you, beckoning you to be one with Him and allow Him inside.

Throughout the Old Testament, God spoke to many in an audible voice.

Adam and Eve were the first to communicate with God.

Abraham was told to take his son Isaac to Mount Sinai and offer him on the altar as an offering to God, and God spoke to him loud and clear just before Abraham killed Isaac, telling him not to do it, after all. Abraham had proven his faithfulness.

Noah was told to build an ark and warned of the coming flood.

Moses was spoken to from a burning bush and told to lead God's people out of bondage and to the land flowing with milk and honey.

Lot was told to take his family from the city of Sodom and Gomorrah and not look back.

Now, you might be saying that those were Bible times, and God doesn't speak like that to people any longer, but that's just not true. God speaks to His children (believers) daily through the Holy Spirit. And whether you believe it or not, sometimes it's even in an audible voice to get our attention.

There have been many debates and controversy over whether God still speaks to people. Non-believers like to think that God never really spoke to anyone, and that the Bible is just a made-up book of fairy tales.

Some Christians believe that you have to be close to God in order to hear Him, and even though they believe that Jesus Christ is their Lord and Savior, they confess that God just doesn't speak to them the way He does others.

The truth is no one is ***more*** saved than any other. When we repent of our sins and ask Jesus to save us, the Holy Spirit takes up residence inside us. He can never leave us nor forsake us after that. We are in Him and He is in us. We don't have to go through years of searching for the closeness to hear His voice; we simply have to listen.

I agree, however, that it is impossible to actually hear Him if our minds are never on Him, just like with the radio station I was speaking of. We need to stay in tune with God.

We hear God's voice by reading His Word. We hear it through worship and prayer. If we never read the Word of God, then we have no idea of His instructions for our life. If we don't pray, then we break our communication with Him. And as we worship Him and allow His sweet Spirit to overflow us, we are able to actually feel His presence and hear His sweet voice.

Have you ever been driving down the road and planning on taking a certain route, and inside your mind you hear, "Turn here," and you find yourself taking another route you never actually planned to take?

Several miles down the road it occurs to you what you just did, and for an instant, you're upset with yourself because you took the long way and wondered what it was that got you off track.

It's so hard for some people to grasp the fact that the Holy Spirit is actually living inside of them. He whispers to you constantly and warns you of things to come. It was His voice that said, "Turn here," and you just turned without even thinking about it.

The Holy Spirit has been called your conscience many times. He's that warning that you should flee, or that thought that maybe you shouldn't be here and about to do something that wouldn't be pleasing to God. He's that still, small whisper that keeps you from so much trouble, if you could just learn to listen to what's inside your heart and head.

****

I once was at a megachurch during praise and worship service when the Holy Spirit spoke to me and said, "Tell that man behind you that if he will do as I have instructed him to do, I will give them their heart's desire." I looked behind me for a moment to see who it was I was supposed to give God's instructions to and saw a couple in their thirties, perhaps, that I had never seen before.

At this time in my life, I was just learning to obey God's voice, and it seemed that He would instruct me to do something daily, maybe just to see if I would.

I kept singing and praising with the music and questioning God in my head. "I don't know these people, Lord, and he will think I have lost my mind."

Again I heard in my spirit, "Tell him what I have instructed, my daughter; he needs to know."

I thought to myself that I would wait until the service was over. The church I was attending at the time held several thousand, and it was a packed house that morning.

I would like to tell you that the moment the service was over, I did just as God commanded, but instead I went downstairs with my husband at the time to get my five-year-old son from Kid-Pack. I had walked away without doing as God told me to do!

As I waited in line, God reminded me and told me to go back. I looked at my husband and said, I'll meet you in the car; there's something I must do, and I started running back as quickly as I could, knowing I had failed God. My mind had gotten wrapped up in the service, and I had completely forgotten to obey God as I promised I would.

Thinking that there was no way the couple behind me was still there, because church had been over for ten minutes by this time, to my amazement, there was no one else in the section I was sitting in but that couple! They were both still there sitting in their seats.

As I started up the steps to the balcony, I saw the man get up and start toward me as if he knew I was coming to speak to him.

"Hello," I said out of breath. "I have something God wants me to tell you."

He smiled and said, "I know. He told me to sit still--that someone was coming back with a message from Him."

"He wants me to tell you that if you will do what He has instructed you to do, He will give you and your wife your hearts' desire."

The man smiled at me as I asked if he knew what it was God wanted him to do. He smiled again and nodded his head yes, and thanked me for coming back.

I went home that day giddy with joy. Not only had the Holy Spirit instructed me what to tell him, He had instructed him to wait on me with a message from Him.

Do you see how God works? He could have just told him what He wanted and not placed me in the middle at all, but by giving this young man a message through a third party, it built both our faith and His message got through.

Several weeks later, I was back again in the same church during praise and worship service, and I noticed the man I had spoken to singing in the choir that morning. It made me happy seeing him up there, and I wondered if this was what God had been speaking of. Had God wanted him to sing in the choir? Or was this just part of God's plan for this man's life?

A month or so after that, there I was again during the service, and as the pastor spoke to the congregation, the Holy Spirit spoke to me. "Tell them both that I am going to bless them with a baby very soon."

I had noticed that the same couple was sitting behind me. There had been no choir that morning, so the man was sitting once again with his wife. I could hardly wait for service to be over to relay this message.

After church was over, I turned around and said," Have you two been wanting a baby?" I saw him look at his wife strangely.

"Yes, in a few years."

I smiled at him and shook my head no. "Well, according to what God is telling me, it will be very soon."

When I was leaving the church, I couldn't help but wonder if the thought had been my own and not His at all.

I really hate when I question God, but as a human I do that often, and He still loves me in spite of it and reminds me to have faith and trust in Him.

Two weeks after that incident, I heard a voice behind me, screaming for me to wait up as I was leaving the church. I turned to see that same man running toward me.

Out of breath, he took my hands and was almost laughing. "When you told us two weeks ago that we were going to have a baby soon, we thought you were crazy, because we had been trying so long to have a baby, and the doctors were afraid my wife couldn't get pregnant, and we were going to try fertility drugs. We stopped on our way home to buy a pregnancy test, and sure enough, she was pregnant. We found out just this week she was two weeks pregnant then, and now she is four weeks!"

I laughed till I cried and hugged him. We serve a mighty God who actually cares about each and every one of us in an amazing way. When he told me to pray that the baby would be okay, I laughed again and reminded him that God had already confirmed it, and there would be nothing wrong with this baby.

God was working in both our lives and teaching us both to trust Him.

****

One day I was driving down highway 129 from Cleveland, Georgia on my way home to Gainesville, when the Holy Spirit spoke to me and told me to go and get my grandmother's armoire that she used to keep her clothes in, because the house was going to burn down. Now, keep in mind that my grandparents had passed away many years ago, and my uncle who lived with them had recently passed, so the big old house was empty. All of us children and grandchildren had already gone through the house and picked out things we wanted by placing our names on them.

I was the only one who still had not gotten my things out, because I had been so busy I had not taken the time to go over and retrieve the things that were to be mine.

As I passed the big old house, I glanced that way and said a silent prayer to God to keep the house safe until I could get over there with a truck and someone to help get the very heavy armoire.

I have to be honest. As always, I questioned God and asked if the thought had been my own or His, and He reminded me that I should get my things soon, because the house was going to burn to the ground. It sickened me to think about it, but now knowing God's voice, I knew I should go very soon.

I went home and told my husband what God had shared with me, and he met me there a week later with his truck and trailer and two of my sons.

After it was loaded, I told them to go home and I would be home a little later. I wanted to once more wander through their old house and reminisce alone.

I stayed about an hour there by myself. Everyone had already gotten everything they wanted, and now it was just pick and grab over what was left.

Another uncle told me they were going to get a huge garbage container and throw the things away before the house was put up for sale, but God told me otherwise. So I went through drawers and found silverware, glasses, and a few pillows grandmother had made and knick-knacks and took them all to my car.

When I was finished, I wandered though the huge old house one more time talking aloud to my grandparents and remembering all the great times I had there as a child growing up. I went home extremely sad that day, but also glad I had listened to God's voice and gotten the things that really meant something to me.

Exactly two weeks from that day, my cousin texted to tell me that my grandparents' house was at that moment burning to the ground. Apparently, a neighbor had seen two strangers running from the house. The fire chief later said it was arson, but as of this day they have never found who deliberately set their house on fire.

God really doesn't care about material things, but He knew how much my grandparents meant to me and that I would be heartbroken if the house burned and I had never gotten the things that I cherished so much.

He warned me because He loved me; that's how much each of us mean to Him. Had He not warned me, I would never have gone over the next week to retrieve my things, and my spirit would have been crushed. Isn't God so amazing?

****

Not long after my ex-husband had left us, I was only making two hundred dollars a week. I was at church one Sunday morning with a twenty-dollar bill in my hand waiting to place it into the offering plate, when the Holy Spirit spoke to me and said, "Don't put that twenty in the offering plate."

I was confused because I believe in paying my tithes, and I know God wants us to place them into the storehouse, which is the church.

I had always placed my tithes into the offering plate, but today He was telling me not to. I stuck the twenty in my pocket and asked Him in my spirit what was I to do with it? He simply answered, "Trust Me."

Within a few seconds, an older man I had never seen before started making his way up the steps toward the balcony in which I sat. Instead of taking a seat, he sat down on the steps just a row down from me. He was dirty, and an unpleasant smell was now all around him.

My heart has always gone out for the homeless. Maybe it was God who placed that he was homeless on my heart, but somehow I just knew.

On that particular Sunday morning, I had an empty seat beside me, and I stood up and took a step down to speak to him. "Would you like to come and sit by me?" I asked.

He smiled at me and did just as I asked. He seemed a bit shocked, for I am sure he knew how unpleasant he smelled and tried to take a seat away from everyone so as not to bother them.

I cannot tell you what the pastor spoke on that Sunday morning as the Holy Spirit was sharing with me this homeless man's story and how special he was to Him. He reminded me of how much He loves all of us, not just some of us, and that He died for all of us and not just some of us.

He shared with me that this stranger made his way to church this morning, and all he desired was to have his spirit fed, but God wanted him to also have his belly fed, and that is why He had told me not to place the twenty in the offering plate.

My son and I were struggling at that time in our life, and it was very hard to live off one hundred eighty dollars a week after I had released my tithes, but God always found a way for me to pay what needed to be paid because I was obedient with them. Had I not been struggling myself, I would love to have given this man more, but all I had was the twenty in my pocket that rightfully belonged to God, and on this day He wanted me to give it to a homeless man and not the storehouse.

I asked God in my spirit as the service continued, how was I going to give it to him? He replied that He would let me know.

Just before the end of the service, the Holy Spirit spoke to me and told me to get it ready by rolling it up and placing it in the palm of my right hand. I did as I was instructed to do.

When we were having altar call, the man stood up and started to leave. Since I was on the end of the row, he had to go by me. I held out my right hand with the twenty rolled up and shook his hand, slipping the twenty into his palm.

"I'm so glad you came to worship with us today; please feel free to come back and sit with me anytime."

He smiled at me, the sweetest smile, and stuck the twenty into his pocket and left without saying a word.

I never saw him after that day, but I have wondered about him from time to time. God always amazes me how He works and how much He truly loves each of us.

****

One day, I was in the line at Walmart and observing an older cashier as she waited on others. She was trying to smile, but I could see in my spirit that there was something wrong with her.

When it was my turn, I looked on her name badge and noticed her name was Lillian. I smiled and said, "Lillian, how are you doing today?"

She tried to smile back and said, "I'm fine, how are you?"

"I'm doing great," I answered, "but I can tell something is wrong. Are you okay?"

She looked at me with tired eyes and began to speak. "You are right. My back is really hurting me today, and I still have several hours to work."

I knew then why God had directed me down Lillian's aisle even though there were others less crowded.

"May I pray for you?" I asked, and held out my hands wanting to take hers.

She placed her hands in mine, and I prayed for God to heal her back, not caring who was around us. When I was finished, she thanked me, and I went on my way, thanking the Holy Spirit for leading me to her, so He might touch her and build her faith. There is no doubt in my mind that her back stopped hurting, and she was able to get through her shift with no more pain.

****

As you are reading this chapter, you might be saying to yourself, wow, that's just how God works with me, or you could be one of many who say God doesn't speak to me like this or has never spoken to me at all.

Maybe deep down you don't even buy into it at all, or maybe you can't understand why God doesn't use you in this way.

Trust me--He truly wants to use all of us that He dwells inside. He wants so desperately to use you for His glory, because there are many lost that only ***you*** can reach. He wants to show you as your teacher what His desire is for your life, but the only way He can do that is for you to dig deep into His Word (through the Holy Bible) and allow Him to guide you through the process. There is absolutely no way you can fully understand what God is saying to you unless you have the knowledge of His Holy Word. His Word is like an instruction manual to each of us, and as we go through our daily lives, He speaks to us by pulling out certain parts of it to remind us of what we are to do or not to do.

It crushes me when I hear people say they don't understand the Bible, and that's why they don't read it. How can one ever understand if you don't constantly read and study? Find a class if you have to, but do what it takes to seek the knowledge of God's Word, His love letter to us all.

I hope you realize that as a Christian it is our gift to Him to allow Him to use us for His glory. He simply cannot use us if we haven't a clue what His desire is for us, and that comes through knowing His Word.

We must realize that most of those thoughts we have, if biblical, are from Him and not our own.

If you feel the Holy Spirit speaking to you, and you question whether it's Him or not, ask yourself if it's biblical. In other words, if you are married and you feel God has sent someone else who can make you happier, that is ***not*** from God. God will not send another person into your life if you are married, because adultery displeases God.

Remember, Satan can also whisper thoughts into your head, and through knowing the Word, you will be able to tell the difference.

****

"Just for the record, if you feel like God spoke something to you and it contradicts what the Bible says, you heard incorrectly; no matter how right something feels, our feelings do not trump with the Word of God.

Pastor Josh Turner

****

If you are one of many who still say they have never heard God speak to them, then I encourage you to start praying and asking Him to reveal Himself to you. Tell Him you are ready and willing to obey Him. Give yourself to Him as a willing vessel, and then give Him the praise and glory He deserves when great things happen. Be careful not to take the credit for His work; He isn't pleased with those who boast.

I'm excited for each of you who are now eager to get started truly listening to God's voice, but not as excited as He is.

Chapter Nine

Studying God's Word

****

It is written that man does not live on bread alone, but on every word that comes from the mouth of God. *(Matthew 4:4) NIV*

****

It is imperative that we go into studying God's Word after the last chapter because it is so important. In fact, studying and learning God's Word is one of the most important things you will ever learn in your life.

Just as I told you in the beginning of this book, you must know and believe that God's Word is truly the Word of God given to men He trusted to pass it along to His creation, so that we may know what His desire is for our life.

God's Word is still the same today as it was over two thousand years ago.

Many have tried to change it by adding to it or taking away from it, but God warns us not to add to or take away from any part of His Word.

****

Do not add to what I command you and do not subtract from it, but keep the commands of the Lord your God that I give. *(Deuteronomy 4:2)NIV*

****

God's word cannot lie. God does not lie, nor has He ever. As the old saying goes, you can take it to the bank, because if God says it, then that settles it.

The more you dig into God's Word, the more He reveals to you, and the closer you become on your walk with Him, and the closer you become to our loving Father, the further away sin will be in your life. You will feel yourself slowly changing from the inside out and others will see the difference in you.

God's Word will truly come alive inside of you, and you will start to speak it in your everyday talk to people.

You will start to view the world differently and understand why people have changed, but God's Word hasn't.

You will slowly pull away from those who go against God's Word without even trying to, and you will hunger to be around those who live it, and you will start to live it also. You'll find yourself doing things and saying things that you would never have dreamed of, and you will be pleased with the person you become because you know God is pleased with you.

There are so many ways one can study the Bible, but whichever way you choose, do not get discouraged and put it down.

I encourage you to start with the New Testament first. The gospels, Matthew, Mark, Luke and John are all recollections of when Jesus lived and walked on the earth. Each book as told by Matthew, Mark, Luke and John consists of the same recollections, just told a bit differently because we all see things differently.

My favorite is John, but it's up to you to pick your favorite.

Study closely the words that Jesus spoke, and if something bothers you or you don't quite understand its meaning, then seek a Bible course in Theology or go to your pastors or the elders of your church. By all means, don't go to someone that you know isn't living right themselves. Make sure the person you ask is filled with the Spirit and the life they live leaves no doubt that they are on fire for God.

If the question you ask cannot be answered by them, then seek even higher. But don't assume no one knows and go on. There is no question too crazy to ask, and asking questions is the way we learn.

Also remember that just because a passage is worded one way doesn't always mean the way it sounds. It is so important to know who wrote the book of the Bible that you are studying. Who were they speaking to at the time? Was it the Jews or the Gentiles, the believers or the non-believers? In what time period did they write it and what were their circumstances? (Most Bibles answer these questions just before the beginning of each book.)

Be sure to invite the Holy Spirit into your Bible reading and studies. Ask Him to open your eyes and help you see what was intended for you to see. Never read the Bible without first praying and seeking God's knowledge. God loves for you to hunger for Him, and He is eager to reveal Himself to you.

As I have stressed in chapter six, it is so important that you stay rooted in a Bible-believing church and attend regularly. And again, by Bible-believing, I mean a church that speaks the whole word, not just parts of it.

By attending church, you will not only be able to worship God, but you will begin to seek the knowledge you long for. You will learn more each week, and like a sponge you will slowly start to absorb the Word more and more.

I stress that you purchase a Bible that you can understand. I know your grandmother's old torn King James Version is a family heirloom and has been carried down through the generations, but place it somewhere safe and purchase a NJKV or an NIV Bible.

Don't be afraid to mark in it. I've heard people say they would never write in their Bible because it is sacred. Trust me, God wants you to tear into His Word, and if making notes all through the pages helps you to learn more, then do it. Just think, in the years to come when your Bible gets passed down through the generations, your family yet to come will have your notes and be able to learn from them also.

Take notes, not just in your Bible, but in a ledger or notebook. Go back and reread your notes from time to time and have them embedded in your brain, so you will be able to pull them back out when you need to share God's Word with others.

When God's Word is truly embedded in your heart and in your mind, never again will you find yourself short on words when someone is questioning God or His existence. You will be more confident and find boldness like never before.

****

I tell you the truth, if anyone keeps My Word, he will never see death. *(John 8:51)NIV*

****

So many times in my life when I was a younger Christian, I allowed people to sway me over to their way of thinking only because I didn't fully understand God's Word. Therefore, I couldn't pull it up and speak it to let them know they were wrong.

Just because this is the 21st century, and so many laws go against God's Word doesn't mean it is okay with God. Remember, God's Word will never change. He is still the same yesterday, today and tomorrow. Nowhere from Genesis through Revelation does it say that these words are only good for so many years. God intended for us to obey His word from the time it was written until the end of time.

I attended the School of Discipleship for three years, and I am now on my second year of Theology, where I plan to take another year at Kineo, Ministry Training Center. Afterwards, six years of my life will have been invested in Biblical studies, and I am sure there will still be certain things I don't quite understand, but I am learning more and more each and every day of my life, through prayer, worship and studying God's Word.

He delights in those who seek Him, and He is so eager to share with you. So many have spent years in school for a profession such as a medical degree or education degree, or so many other degrees that are offered, and hold back on studying God's Word, saying there just isn't any time left in their schedules, when as I said in the past chapter, studying and learning what's in God's Word is the most important thing you can ever learn on this earth. So go after it. Find someplace close or seek online and start taking a course in Biblical studies. I promise you that you will never regret it.

****

If you are interested in attending Kineo (to move) Ministry Training Center under the leadership and teaching of Pastor Karen Smith, it is offered online at: www.KINEOMTC.com because every Christian needs to be equipped to do the work of the ministry, to move forward.

I can assure you that you will be amazed at how the Bible will come alive when learning from someone who truly knows and understands God's Word.

Pastor Karen Smith has spent most of her life studying and researching God's Word and is a delight to learn from.

For those who live close enough and like a hands-on, classroom setting, Kineo Ministry Training Center is located at 139 Hightower Parkway, Dawsonville, Georgia 30534.

Chapter Ten

Become a Prayer Warrior

****

If My people, who are called by My name, will humble themselves and pray and seek My face and turn from their wicked way, then I will hear from heaven and I will forgive their sin and heal their land. *(2 Chronicles 7:14) NIV*

****

Let me start by asking you an important question. I want you to think about your prayer life. How strong is it? There are four types of Christians when it comes to prayer.

1. Those who pray daily at certain times, either morning when they arise or right before they close their eyes at night, or both.
2. Those who pray only when they have strife in their life, or are struggling through a storm, a bad period in which they see no way out but with God.
3. Those who pray not only at certain times throughout the day but pray repetitious prayers, always using the same words each time and never truly opening up their heart to God.

4. Those who continuously pray throughout the day whether aloud or silent, and are always speaking to the Holy Spirit within them and seeking His guidance or simply thanking Him for His blessings.

****

If you are anything but number four, then your prayer life needs help. God's desire is that we continuously stay in prayer with Him, and seek His guidance in our everyday walk with Him. This doesn't mean we have to stay on our knees 24/7. It simply means that we acknowledge the Holy Spirit within us and speak to Him regularly as we would our best friend who hangs out with us for the day.

If your best friend came to hang out with you for an entire day, would you ignore that they were there? Of course you wouldn't. So, knowing that after you are saved, the Holy Spirit has moved in and taken up residence inside you, why would you go a long period of time without speaking to Him?

I am sure there have been times in your life when you felt God was a million miles away. Life can be hard at times, and always at those moments you question God, wanting to know where He was throughout all of it.

The truth is He was right where He has always been; it was ***you*** who drifted from Him. When the Bible stated that He will never leave you nor forsake you, it wasn't lying. Remember, God cannot tell a lie, so therefore He can never leave you once He has moved in. The Holy Spirit, who is a part of God, moves in the day you are saved and your eternity starts from that moment.

Trust me, after that, He speaks to you daily, trying His best to guide and direct your life, warning you of things and doing everything possible to keep you from harm. The problem is that so many people just simply do not listen. They choose to go through each day on their own, never asking for God's help whatsoever, until they fall flat on their face and realize they can't do it on their own, and then it's, "Help me, Lord, where have You been?"

So many times God gets the blame for things that we allowed to happen to ourselves. God did not give you all those cigarettes you smoked daily, which caused you to have lung cancer or COPD, and now in your later years, you are on oxygen and can hardly talk for coughing.

God didn't give you the alcohol you consumed so much of that caused you to develop liver poisoning.

God didn't hand you the drugs you took so willingly that caused your children to be taken away, and now you are left feeling empty inside.

Believe it or not, God didn't even give you cancer, and He hates that you have it at all, but He has the ability to heal you, and many times He does. There are also times when He steps back and allows you to go through it, in order to get you or someone around you to where you need to be in Him.

God's plans are not always our plans, but if we trust in Him and allow Him to use whatever the situation is for His glory, He will turn a bad situation around and something good will come out of it.

So it's time to stop blaming God for everything that happens in your life and believing that it was in God's plan, because so much of what you do each day wasn't His plan at all. He only wants good for His children, just as you want good for your own children.

Start thanking Him daily for everything. Just waking up each day is such a blessing. He gave you another day to live on this earth, on this side of heaven, so that you might serve Him another day.

When your prayer life grows, you grow. The more you read God's Word and pray continuously asking His guidance for everything, the more you will hear His voice. The three go together and it's hard to have one without the other. In fact, it's almost impossible.

When someone asks you to pray for them, do you simply reply that you will or do you take their hand and pray at that moment? If you read on Facebook that someone is requesting prayer, do you click the like button and comment praying and then never really pray at all?

How many times has someone asked you to pray, and you forgot about their request the moment you said you would? I've actually been guilty of this, and when I remember, it shames me and I have to stop and pray.

Ask yourself if you are even someone that people would ask to pray for them or pray over a certain situation. If no one has ever asked you, then you need to ask yourself how others perceive you.

Think about the people you know. If you desperately needed prayer, which ones would you go to? You would go to the people you thought might be able to get a prayer through to God, the ones that you could see had really lived a life pleasing to God, so that God would honor their prayer.

The last people you would go to for prayer are the ones that you know live a life unpleasing to God, or are living in sin daily.

So again I ask you, are you someone people ask to pray for them? How many times, thinking back, have people asked you to pray for them or someone they knew who needed prayer? If no one ever has, it might be a good time to strive to become a person people would come to for prayer.

Many fail to pray aloud for others because they find it uncomfortable. There is nothing more uncomfortable than to be asked to pray aloud or lead a prayer when you're not used to ever doing it. I used to be in the same boat with you in my younger years when I was a shy teenager. I'd just as soon drop dead right there on the spot as to be placed in the spotlight of leading a prayer. After all, what would I say, and would they think I was crazy? Would I stumble over my words and find myself speechless? Well, trust me--I have at first, many times.

The more I found myself praying aloud at home in private, the easier it became to pray aloud in front of others.

*****

For where two or three are gathered together in My name, there I am in the midst of them. *(Matthew 18:20) KJV*

****

When we first meet someone, we have this incredible desire to communicate with them. As women, we find ourselves getting upset with our husbands if they come in and would rather watch the television or get preoccupied and ignore us.

We long for conversation and eat up the attention that our spouses give us. Don't you think that God desires that same attention from His believers?

The day that you accepted Him into your life was like the day you married your spouse. You promised God that you would live for Him and serve Him and accepted His gift of eternal life, just as you accepted your spouse's ring around your finger committing your life to them forever.

Chapter Eleven

Lead, not Follow

****

For some people we are the only avenue to God, make sure the road is free of debris.

Pastor Todd Smith

****

Somewhere in your life someone has told you whether you are a leader or a follower. It was probably your parents when you were much younger, and they probably stressed to you that you should be an example to others and stop hanging around friends who would lead you down the wrong road.

Being a follower doesn't diminish with age. In fact, if you were a follower when you were young, it probably followed you into adulthood.

It isn't always easy saying no to your friends who have been there since childhood, especially if you feel you are doing nothing wrong by hanging out in bars on Friday and Saturday nights. After all, you aren't harming anyone, right?

In previous chapters, I have said numerous times that once we are saved, we have the Holy Spirit living inside of us. We then become the body of Christ. He is in us and we are in Him.

With that being said and knowing this is a fact, it proves that we take the Holy Spirit wherever we go. If we go out to a bar on Friday or Saturday night, He is there also because we took Him there.

If we cheat on our spouse and think that by meeting them somewhere out of town and private no one will see, we are wrong. We have taken Him right to the hotel room with us. He watches everything we do. And I do mean ***everything***.

When we tell our parents we are spending the night at a friend's house and really went to a party down the street where drugs and alcohol are, we have taken the Holy Spirit with us.

He sees us when we sleep with men or women we aren't married to, and He sees us when we lose our temper and use words that are displeasing to Him.

Trust me, since I have been saved and housing the Holy Spirit from the age of eleven, I have taken Him many places that have grieved Him, and because of that, I am ashamed, but because He loves me unconditionally, He loved me through it all and I have now been forgiven.

I have never been one to drink, nor have I ever done any drugs, but I still fell short in many areas of my life.

I was never a follower because I always had the will power to say no, but because I went through so much of my life feeling ugly, I had the desire to feel beautiful and be needed by men who were no good for me.

So many of us do things that are displeasing to God and somehow make ourselves feel justified, thinking we are good in other areas of our life. The truth is, as I said before, if it goes against God's Word, it's just plain wrong!

I even told my children once, because of a divorce I'd been through, that they should live with someone before they married them to make sure before they made a mistake.

Do you see how I led my children to believe something that wasn't true? I was guilty of leading them away from God and went against the Bible when God's Word clearly says that fornication is a sin.

When we want to do something displeasing to God, we justify ourselves by saying that God loves us so much He would want me to be sure before I got married. We tell ourselves that our good outweighs our bad, and therefore God doesn't mind this one little thing, or that we can always ask forgiveness for it later, right? Oh, how many times I have been there and done that.

I have found out something very important throughout my life, though, and that is we will surely reap the seeds we sow. Every choice you make is a seed you sow. We are the product of our choices.

****

Do not be deceived. God cannot be mocked. A man reaps what he sows. The one who sows to please his sinful nature, from that nature will reap destruction; the one who sows to please the Spirit, from that Spirit will reap eternal life. *(Galatians 6:7-8)NIV*

****

One of the most crucial mistakes we can make is following our feelings and our emotions instead of following God's Word. (Another reason we must have Bible knowledge.) If God's Word goes against it, then don't do it, period. It's that simple.

It's okay to wait for sex after marriage. In fact, that is God's desire for us. It's okay to say no to drugs and alcohol and stay away from places where you know you shouldn't be. If you are headed to a place you wouldn't want your children, your parents or your pastor to see you, then why in this world would you take the Holy Spirit there?

Even though I was a leader, I have not always led in the right direction. Now that I am older and deeper in my walk with Christ, I can look back over my life and see where I went wrong. Each time I wasn't reading my Bible, I only prayed when I needed something major, and I paused from church for a while.

To be a true leader who is pleasing to God and walk a Christian life where people actually see that you are a man or woman of God, you have to learn to step up and step out, standing up for what the Bible teaches us through God's Word.

God wants you to be a leader, but His desire is for you to lead people to Him, not lead them astray. I've thought many times I wish I had another shot at raising my children. Oh, how I would do a few things differently.

Leaders lead by example, and this is the same with God. To lead someone to Christ, you have to first be Christlike yourself. When you allow God to work through you to fulfill His purposes, He wants you to be walking as closely to Him as possible. You cannot lead people to Christ and be living out in sin; it just doesn't work that way.

Because this is the 21st century and so many of our laws have changed, many have now changed their minds about what they used to believe because God was against it. So many denominations are upholding the law instead of upholding God's Word, and the Bible does warn us of this in Revelation.

God foresaw thousands of years ago that one day many of His children would step out of the will of God and believe things to be okay simply because it was pleasing to others. Take homosexuality, for instance. The Bible tells us all throughout the Bible that homosexuality is a sin and is an abomination of hell and He detests it, yet because our government now says it is okay for the same sex to unite in marriage, many churches are now marrying people of the same sex.

Tell me, how would God be okay with this when He destroyed an entire city for that same exact thing? It wasn't God who changed His mind; it was us to suit our needs and desires.

Since God called homosexuality perversion, it proves you are not created or born as a homosexual. Instead, we are created in His image, and His desire is for marriage to be between one man and one woman.

I have many homosexual friends that I love very much, and I don't treat them any differently than I treat anyone else. God desires for us to love everyone just as He loves, but if asked I would say it is wrong because it goes against God's Word, and trust me, my friends know how I feel about it. I don't criticize them or belittle them or shy away from them. Instead, I continue to let my light shine for God, knowing how much God loves them despite their sin.

****

The same holds true with abortion. Because it is lawful, many Christians believe that a woman has the right to choose, but the Bible tells us that God knew us even before we were in our mother's womb.

****

Before I formed you in your mother's womb I knew you. Before you were born I set you apart. *(Jeremiah 1:5)*

****

This is a subject on which I have had many people come against me and want to argue their beliefs, and many of them are Christians. I am still confused by how anyone would think it is okay to kill an unborn baby when all creation comes from God.

I've even known a couple of women who have had two or three abortions and think nothing of it. It's like they think, I didn't mean to get pregnant, and I don't really want a child, so let's just go down to the clinic and have it removed.

****

This day I call heaven and earth as witnesses against you that I have set before you life and death, blessings and curses. Now choose LIFE, so that you and your children may live. *(Deuteronomy 30:19)*

****

It literally makes me sick to my stomach when I think about partial-birth abortion and how, because the law has changed even more, so many think it's okay to kill a baby just days before it's born when the baby is considered full-term.

Nothing will make me change my mind on this subject, and I will continue to be a voice for the unborn for as long as God allows me on this earth.

What truly surprises me is that many Christians believe in same-sex marriages but don't believe in abortion, or they believe in abortion but not same-sex marriages. I'll say it again, if it is wrong in God's Word, it is wrong, period.

Stop trying to justify what you or others are doing and be a leader who will lead people to Christ.

Say to yourself, is what I am about to do or say pleasing to God? Does what I am about to do or say go against God's Word? If the answer is yes, refrain from doing or saying it, and each day try to be better than the day before.

We all make mistakes, but when we find ourselves making the same mistakes over and over, it becomes a choice.

If, at this moment, you are feeling a little lost, or maybe you are thinking, who am I to lead people to Christ, I'm here to tell you it doesn't matter if you're a pastor, evangelist or missionary. You don't have to have a biblical title, because God doesn't care what your credentials are. We are all here for the same purpose, and that is to lead others to Christ through different gifts. God works with each of us differently under different circumstances, but He fully expects us to live each day knowing our purpose is to allow Him to work through us and be a willing vessel for Him.

Maybe you blew it in years past just as I have, and that's okay. Today is a brand-new day filled with brand-new beginnings, and God is waiting for the leader inside you to come forth and lead His people who have gone astray.

Chapter Twelve

Never Give Up

****

Everything is possible for him who believes. *(Mark 9:23)*

****

If I had given up on my dream from the age of nine to be a writer, you wouldn't be reading this now or any other book that has my name on it.

God gives us dreams and desires for us to pursue them by going after them full-force. Sometimes it isn't easy making our dreams become reality, but if we give up, the dream dies. Only we can achieve our dreams; no one else cares more about them than we do.

****

One day, not so long ago, I was in a step contest with one of my best friends, and I decided I'd go walking around my subdivision. I had worked many hours that week and had no time for exercise such as walking.

I had just started out and had not gotten far from my front door when it began to downpour. My first thought was to turn around and run back to the safety of my front porch, where I knew I would be dry and find shelter.

If you know me at all, you know how I hate to be rained on. In fact, I will refrain from going somewhere if I think it is going to rain, just to keep from getting my hair wet.

On this particular day, as I started to turn and head for my house, the Holy Spirit spoke to me and said, "Keep going."

Now why in this world did the Holy Spirit desire for me to become dripping wet? What could His purpose be? That was certainly not a plan I was happy with, but again I heard Him tell me to keep going, and so I sighed heavily and continued on my walk.

For the next fifteen minutes, it rained so hard I could barely see. Many times I had to stop and clear away the water from my eyes, so I could see how to continue on.

When the rain finally stopped, I was far away from the house and was soaked completely through, every inch of my clothing. My hair, which I hate getting wet, was stuck to me like glue, and I am sure my makeup had completely washed off.

"Now, what was that all about?" I asked the Holy Spirit, trying to squeeze the water from my now-soaked shirt.

"There's a lesson to be learned here, my daughter. Thank you for not giving up."

I had to giggle at the sight of me. It's just like my Father God to try to teach me a valuable life lesson and have fun with it in the process.

Before I made it home, the sun was shining once again, and He reminded me that there is always sunshine after each storm, and as long as we never give up, He will bless us.

****

After Noah had built the ark and Noah's family was safely on land again, God placed a rainbow in the sky as a sign that He would never again destroy the world with water. What if Noah had given up on the ark, even though it took him 120 years to finish it? None of us would be here today; think about it.

Think of all the things we have today as modern-day conveniences. What if the people who discovered them had given up and quit? Would we have the telephone or cell phones? Would we have electricity or heating and air, or what about the automobile? Someone, somewhere, throughout the course of time had a dream and pursued it. And since the Bible tells us God gives us dreams and visions, then God must really love us to have created in the minds of His children what to pursue so we could have so much.

Even though He wants each of us to lead people toward Him, he uses each of us differently according to our gifts.

What is your gift? What dream or vision has been placed inside of you that you haven't yet gone after, because maybe you think it's too hard or uncomfortable? Maybe you feel it is bigger than you.

****

Because you have so little faith, I tell you the truth, if you have faith as small as a mustard seed, you can say to this mountain, 'Move from here to there' and it will move. Nothing will be impossible for you. *(Matthew 17:20) NIV*

****

Remember, Noah was just a common man who loved God, and He and his children built the ark. Creation started all over again because of Noah and his family.

Moses stuttered, and yet he led God's people out of bondage.

David killed a giant, and he didn't need to know Goliath's strength, because he knew God's.

Jacob wrestled with an angel all night because he wanted to be blessed.

****

When we get stale and stop going after that thing God placed on our hearts, we begin to die a slow death without even realizing it.

Don't let the roadblocks keep you from arriving at your destination. There is always a way, when God is at the center.

****

We must go through many hardships to enter the kingdom of God. *(Acts 14:22)NIV*

****

Perhaps you placed your dream on the back burner and cut it on low. Maybe it's time to turn up the heat and ask God to help you.

No matter how dark your start, don't let it diminish your finish. Go after your dreams, especially if you know they were placed there by God and can touch or bless the lives of others. It always takes that first step before you can walk a mile.

****

There are sixteen things that are growth killers in individuals. See if one of these applies to you.

1. I can't.
2. I'll do it later.
3. I can't afford it.
4. Not now.
5. I don't have the time.
6. It's not for me.
7. I'm too young or too old.
8. I have too many children.
9. I need to but.......
10. Tomorrow.
11. I will eventually.
12. Someday I'll......
13. When I can, I will......
14. Next week.
15. Next month.
16. Next year.

All of these things hold you back from going after that thing God placed within you. Just remember, though, that the power of ***yes*** changes everything!

****

I am the light of the world; whoever follows me will never walk in darkness, but will have the light of life. *(John 8:12)NIV*

Chapter Thirteen

Standing Up for Your Beliefs

****

For although they knew God, they neither glorified Him as God nor gave thanks to Him, but their thinking became futile and their foolish hearts were darkened. Although they claimed to be wise, they became fools, and exchanged the glory of the immortal God of images made to look like mortal man and birds and animals and reptiles. Therefore God gave them over to sinful desires of their hearts to sexual impurity for the degrading of their bodies with one another. They exchanged the truth of God for a lie; and worshipped and served created things rather than the creator. Who is forever praised. Amen.

Because of this God gave them over to shameful lusts. Even their women exchanged natural relations for unnatural ones. In the same way the men also abandoned natural relations with women and were inflamed with lust for one another. Men committed indecent acts with other men, and received in themselves the due penalty for their perversions. *(Romans 1:21-27)*

****

As you can see in the verses above, God is against homosexuality. It was important for me to place in this chapter because it has everything to do with standing up for what you believe in.

The world has changed since the Bible days, but again I want to remind you that God's word will always remain the same, no matter how many more thousands of years mankind will endure until the end of time.

We all fall short of the glory of God, and no man other than Jesus ever led a perfect life, but to say we all sin, yet sin differently, is like giving a free pass to sin itself.

Even though God forgives us of our sin and was the sole purpose of Jesus dying on the cross, God dislikes when we deliberately sin knowing we are doing wrong. God's grace declares believers righteous through faith.

****

For all have sinned and fall short of the glory of God, and are justified freely by His grace, through redemption that came through Jesus Christ. *(Romans 3:23-24)*

****

Romans is the best book for Christianity 101. While studying it, don't allow it to scare you, but instead learn what is pleasing and displeasing to God. Many of your questions covering sin will be covered in the book of Romans.

Jesus didn't say follow Christians, he said, "Follow Me."

This chapter coincides with chapter eleven, Lead, not Follow. In order to be a leader, you must stand up for your beliefs. If you agree with someone's sin just to keep from hurting them or causing them to be upset with you, then you have grieved God.

Sometimes you may be the only one that a person who is sinning can actually look up to, and you may be just what they need to lead them back to God. You don't have to be hateful or rude or cast stones, but instead be kind and loving and gently explain why God says what they are doing is wrong by showing them verses that prove what you are saying to be true.

There may be times you may have to pull yourself away from certain people, because they cause you more harm than good, spiritually. It's okay to love them and walk away. It's okay to agree to disagree, also.

I would rather stand by God and be judged by the world, than stand with the world and be judged by God.

There were many times, in my younger walk with Christ, that I agreed with the crowd just to save face, but I can no longer be that kind of Christian.

There will come a time, and hopefully it is now while you are reading this book, that you finally decide that, no matter what comes at you, you will always place God's Word first above anything that others might be doing.

People who live in deliberate sin want to think that God is okay with their sin, so they want others to think it is okay also, but if God was against it in His Word, then He is still against it. God will never, ever change His mind.

****

Therefore, my dear brothers, stand firm. Let nothing move you. Always give yourself fully to the work of the Lord, because you know that your labor in the Lord is not in vain. *(1 Corinthians 15:58)*

****

How is it possible to lead a sinful man back to Christ or to Christ if you agree with His sin? If you are someone he looks up to, and you think it's right, then by all means, it must be right, and instead of leading someone toward God, you willingly lead them further away.

****

Be on your guard; stand firm in the faith; men of courage; be strong. Do everything in love. *(1 Corinthians 16:13)*

****

To walk as Christ walked and live a life pleasing to God, you must say, act and do the things Jesus would have done.

Even though Jesus loved everyone, He wasn't afraid to tell the lady at the well she was sinning when he brought up the men she slept with who weren't her husbands. He called her out and told her to go and sin no more, which meant He forgave her but expected her to go forth and live a life more pleasing to God.

Remember, a gentle word turns away wrath. You can say the same thing and say it in love, and it will have more power behind your words than being hateful and rude. Besides, no one wants to listen to a know-it-all or a one-upper, someone who thinks they are better than others. It's all in the attitude.

Pray each day not only for wisdom to know God's Word, but for courage to always stand up for God's Word. You never know if your gentle leading and kind ways will be the very thing a person needs to hear at that moment that will cause their heart to think differently.

****

Basically, after you learn God's Word, and it gets embedded in your heart, no one will be able to sway you to their way of thinking.

As I've said in a previous chapter, you cannot stand up for God's Word if you don't have Bible knowledge. Now do you see how truly important this is?

Don't ever be ashamed of standing up for what you know to be true and what is pleasing to God, no matter what. This goes for so many things throughout the Bible; some you may have even done in the past, but that's okay. God will take your past and wash it white as snow.

Also, in order to stand up for God's Word, it's good to be living Christlike yourself. No one likes for you to point out their sin when you have present deliberate sin in your own life. Trust me; they will be quick to point it out.

But if it is something that is in your past before your salvation or even after, but you have repented and are now standing on a more solid foundation with God, it's okay to say, "You are right, but I am no longer that person any longer. I was wrong, and I have been forgiven."

I am not saying to jump down someone's throat pointing out their sin. We are to love people, no matter what their sin is. I am merely saying not to agree with them, and if God leads you to speak, then He will lead your words. (This is why it is good to know when the Holy Spirit is speaking to you.)

Chapter Fourteen

Getting Rid of the Junk

****

Submit yourself therefore to God, Resist the Devil; and he will flee from you. *(James 4:7)NIV*

****

We all have baggage. By baggage, I mean things in our past we are not pleased with. I know I certainly have.

When we come to know or decide to recommit our life to God, we are to leave that baggage behind us, never to pick it up again.

But what about the life you live today? For many years of my life, I lived knowing I was doing things that didn't please God or went against the will of God, and I did them as a Christian, because if you remember I was only eleven when I was saved.

I am grateful that the Holy Spirit was still with me and forgave me when I fell on my knees and realized how wrong I had been on so many issues.

It's easy to get caught up in the world and live a life that displeases God. What's bad is when you go through life thinking that you aren't doing anything wrong, and the days become weeks, the weeks, months and the months, years. Then you find yourself looking back and think what just happened? Did I do that?

****

But each person is tempted when he is lured by his own desire. *(James 1:14)NIV*

****

Do you ever wonder how much of what weighs you down is not yours to carry? God has incredible plans for you. Don't waste your tomorrows by chasing after what doesn't even matter.

****

First of all, I need you to understand that ***your*** body is God's temple. We are to protect that temple and be good to it. When you became saved and the Holy Spirit moved in, you became a temple of God.

Picture a temple that people would go to and worship in. Picture yourself as the caregiver of that temple. God has placed you in charge of what He finds to be beautiful and you now have the responsibility to see that it stays beautiful by keeping the lawn mowed around it and flowers watered and shrubs cut.

The inside of this glorious temple must stay clean and free of debris. The floor must stay vacuumed and the benches polished. Your job as temple keeper is not an easy one, but you must do your best, because after all, God placed you in charge of it.

This is the same with your body. You are in charge of your very own temple. What you do with it reflects God after you are saved. Remember, He is in you and you are in Him, so you are now one with the Holy Spirit.

I challenge you to go stand in front of a mirror. Look at yourself. What does your temple look like? Is it a temple in which people would want to come and worship? Has it been nicely kept or does it lack much to be desired?

What habits do you hang onto that cause your temple to run down? What can you give up to improve your temple? Do you smoke or consume too much alcohol? Do you do drugs, whether it's hard drugs or smoke pot? Do you overeat or not eat enough? Do you let yourself go?

All of these things I have mentioned harm your temple, and it is more difficult for God to use a temple that is not up to par.

How would it look to non-Christians if you stood there telling them about God with a joint hanging out of your mouth?

If you had an interview with a very well-known company, knowing that if you were hired you would make a six-figure income and your family would be set for life, how would you present yourself at this interview?

You would dress up in your Sunday best, of course, and leave all habits at the door. You would want your soon-to-be boss to see you as flawless, a man or woman capable of the job.

So why would you come before God any less? Think about it, this is God we are speaking of, the Great Almighty, the one and only, the Savior of all men. Look what He did for you.

****

Don't you know that you yourself are God's temple and that God's Spirit lives in you? If anyone destroys God's temple, God will

destroy him; for God's temple is sacred, and you are that temple. *(1 Corinthians 3:16-17)NIV*

****

This doesn't mean that God will send down a lightning bolt and destroy you, even though He certainly could. It means He will step back and allow you to destroy yourself. In other words, don't cry out to God to help you when you got yourself into that shape to begin with.

Our spirit (if we are in Christ and He is in us) is in constant battle with our flesh. We are to live by the Spirit, so we do not gratify the desires of sinful nature.

The acts of sinful nature are listed in Galatians, Chapter Five. I will list them for you and explain what each one means.

The acts of sinful nature are obvious:

1. **Sexual Immorality**- In the New Testament, the word most often translated "sexual immorality" is *porneia,* this word is also translated as "whoredom," "fornication,"and "idolatry,"it means "a surrendering of sexual purity," and it is primarily used of premarital sexual relations. From this Greek word we get the English word *pornography*, stemming from the concept of "selling off." Sexual immorality is the "selling off" of sexual purity and involves any type of sexual expression outside the boundaries of a biblically-defined marriage relationship. (Matthew 19:4-5)
2. **Impurity**- It is the state of being impure, meaning uncleanness. The Hebrew word of Impurity is *"tumah."* Not being pure.

3. **Debauchery**- Debauchery is the habitual and unrestrained indulgence of lust and sensuality. There are several places in scripture where the word *debauchery* is used to indicate what we today would call "partying." It encompasses several aspects of unholy living, including, but not limited to sexual immorality, drunkenness, crude talk, and generally out-of-control behavior.
4. **Idolatry**- "Worship or reverence given to any created object or person." It actually takes many forms, not just the "praying to statues," that you think of when you hear the word *Idolatry. Fetishism (Fetish,* is derived from the Latin word *factitius,* meaning to *make* – ironically the word *fact* originated from the same Latin word) is when "any living or inanimate object is regarded with awe and devotion." While thousands of everyday things and habits can be included in this category, *especially if they get in the way of one's obedience to, and worship of, the one True God,* statues and religious images are the most common and obvious examples.
5. **Witchcraft**- The scriptures condemn all sorcery as opposed to a proper sense of dependence upon God. In *Galatians 5:20,* witchcraft is listed as being one of the acts of sinful nature.
6. **Hatred**- That which is directed against others. The Lord mentions hatred in the Sermon on the Mount. "***But I tell you that anyone who is angry with his brother will be subject to judgment.***" (Matthew 5:22). The Lord commands that not only should we be reconciled with our brother before we go before the Lord, but also do it quickly. (Matthew

5:23-26). Hatred is a "heart" sin and any hateful thought or act is an act of murder in God's eyes for which justice will be demanded, possibly not in this life but at the judgment.

7. **Discord**- Disagreement among persons, differences of opinions, variance, opposition, strife, any disagreement which produces angry passions, contests, disputes, litigation or war. *Discord* may exist between families, parties and nations.
8. **Jealousy**- Is the suspicion of a wife's purity, one of the strongest passions. (Numbers 5:14; Proverbs 6:34) Also an intense interest of another's honor or prosperity. (Psalms 79:5; 1Corinthians 10;22; Zechariah 1:14)
9. **Fits of Rage**- Do not give in to anger, or be quick to anger. ***Man's anger does not bring about the righteous life that God desires***. (James 1:20)
10. **Selfish Ambition**- Can be characterized as a lifestyle based on "get" – which typically uses and disregards others on a quest to advance the self. Satan is a prime example of this attitude, which is also human work of the flesh. He allowed his pride and violent discontentment to alter his mind into actually thinking he should rule in place of God. (Isaiah 14:13)
11. **Dissensions**- Disagreement in opinion, usually a disagreement which is violent, producing warm debates or angry words, contention in words, strife, discord, quarrel, breach of friendship or union.
12. **Factions**- tumult, discord, dissensions. One that seeks power, usually through intrigue. A dissenting clique.

13. **Envy**- The Greek word translated *envy* means to "burn with zeal." Literally the sense is "to be heated or to boil over with envy, hatred or anger." In the context of (1 Corinthians 13) the idea is that love does not focus on personal desires. It is not eager to increase possessions. God's type of love is selfless, not selfish.
14. **Drunkenness**- The Greek word *methuo* means to be filled, rushed (with liquid), saturated, or satiated. The word can refer to one that fills himself with alcoholic drink.
15. **Orgies**- A wild gathering marked by promiscuous sexual activity, excessive drinking. An act of immoderate or frenzied indulgence. Having more than one sexual partner at a time.

****

Therefore do not let sin reign in your mortal body so that you obey its evil desires. Do not offer the parts of your body to sin, as instruments of wickedness, but rather offer yourselves to God as those who have been brought from death to life; and offer the parts of your body to Him as instruments of righteousness. For sin shall not be your master, because you are not under law, but under grace. *(Romans 6: 11-14)NIV*

****

God is a good God, but He is also a just God. We cannot keep living a life that displeases Him and think that He loves you so much that He will just look over your faults. He clearly gives you a list in His Word of the things that He will put up with and the things He won't.

My children have said, "But Mom, you did this or that, so how can you say now that this is wrong?" It's okay to admit to our children that we were wrong. I confess I was wrong about so many things in my life, and when I look back, I see that I was wrong because I did not know or understand God's Word the way God desired.

I also admit I was afraid to read God's Word for fear that I would stumble on something I was doing, and if I didn't know it was wrong, then how can it be wrong?

The truth is whether we know it or not, it's still wrong. Just because we may not know one plus one equals two, it's still two.

When someone wants to argue about God's Word and try to justify the things they desire to do that are clearly wrong to God, it is because they have no desire to stop that thing they are doing.

They go through life as I did for so many years, thinking there will be time later to change their ways, but what if later doesn't come, and today is all you have?

If you knew that today would be the last day you are given on this earth and tonight you would meet Jesus face to face, would you live today any differently than you did yesterday?

Habits are hard to break and even harder alone. When we lay our habits at the foot of the cross and ask God to take them from us, He will. But it is up to us to leave them at the foot of the cross and vow to never pick them up again.

I know a wonderful Christian lady who smoked cigarettes all of her life and throughout her pregnancies. This was back when people didn't realize they were so harmful to your health. When all the statistics came out and the surgeon general told people that smoking was bad for your health and second-hand smoke was even worse, she was already hooked and would argue if anyone brought it up.

I loved her and only wanted the best for her, but because her mother passed away at the age of fifty-two of lung cancer and never smoked a day in her life, she felt justified to smoke, saying that if she was going to die of lung cancer it wouldn't matter whether she smoked or not.

Today, as I write this, she suffers daily with COPD, and is on oxygen 24/7. Her oxygen level is so low that it causes her to be very feeble and bruise easily. She spends most of her time in bed now, and when she is up she uses a walker.

At seventy-five years old, this once-vibrant woman who traveled with a gospel group and played the banjo and guitar and sang such beautiful songs she had written herself can no longer do the things she desires.

I remember as a young girl she had such endurance to get up early in the morning and hoe in the fields until sundown. She was one of the hardest-working women I have ever known, but today she struggles just to make it to the bathroom.

It's so easy to justify bad habits when you are younger, like smoking cigarettes or pot, or consuming more alcohol than you should.

It's easy to get wrapped up in drugs and become so addicted you can't stop, no matter how hard you try.

For many, the struggle is weight gain. As we get older, our metabolism slows and because we choose unhealthy eating, the weight creeps up until we tell ourselves enough is enough and then struggle to lose it.

All of these things harm the temple of God. But what about the things that hinder you from fully giving yourself to Him, like pornography?

Pornography is a huge industry that makes its money from everyday, normal hard-working people who get wrapped up and consumed in this horrible addiction.

Almost every home in America now has the internet at their fingertips, and with Google and many other search engines, you can put in just one word and bam!! You get lured in to places God never intended you to be.

It starts off with just a sight or two, and pretty soon you spend hours at the computer fantasizing and having impure thoughts. It doesn't take long to become a full-blown addiction, and your mind goes from the things that are pleasing to God to lust.

When you open up a window and allow Satan to come in, He then tempts you even more. Impure thoughts can cause a world of trouble, from fornication to adultery, which can cause you to lose your entire family and everything you love, and leave you feeling empty inside.

Satan is on every corner, luring Christians to turn away from God and choose the road most-traveled. While it may seem like fun and excitement at the time, it won't accomplish anything but grief later on.

****

It is for freedom that Christ has set us free. Stand firm, then, and do not let yourselves be burdened again by a yoke of slavery. *(Galatians 5:1)NIV*

****

When we choose to keep the junk in our lives, we become a slave to it. There is just no way you can live a life pleasing to God and lead other people toward Him and hang on to the junk and the bad habits.

Smoking cigarettes didn't make this great woman a bad person, but because she chose to hang on to it, it harmed her temple and now she suffers greatly.

Evaluate your life and the things you put inside God's temple (your body) and ask yourself if there is anything you need to do differently and then start today.

For some, just placing it at the foot of the cross is all that is needed. When you truly give it to God and ask for His help and stay around people who love you and care about you, you will see a change in the way you view things.

For others, professional help may be needed, and don't be afraid to seek it. Some things are too big to handle alone, and not everyone's strengths are the same.

Chapter Fifteen

Tithing

****

You shall remember the Lord your God, for it is He who gives you power to get wealth, that He may confirm His covenant that He swore to your fathers, as it is this day. *(Deuteronomy 8:18)*

****

I know a pastor personally who said God no longer expects us to tithe, but that simply isn't true.

If you are under the assumption that just because the church is God's house He will take care of it, you are under the wrong assumption. God is under no obligation to bless the church. It is up to us to tithe as He commanded.

If you have no idea what I am speaking of, let me explain. Paying your tithes means to give 10% of your gross pay each week (or whenever you get your paycheck) back to God.

****

Give to Caesar what is Caesar's and God what is God's. (Matthew 22:21)NIV

****

Paying your tithes is a requirement of God. He doesn't want you to pay if you can afford it; He wants you to pay your tithes first before anything else, and He will see that all your needs are met. In other words, He wants you to trust Him, and when He sees that He can trust you with little, then He will bless you with more.

****

Whosoever can be trusted with very little can be trusted with much, and whosoever is dishonest with very little will be dishonest with much. So if you have not been trustworthy in handling worldly wealth, who will trust you with true riches? And if you have not been trustworthy with someone else's property, who will give you property of your own? *(Luke 16:10–12)NIV*

****

How can we ask God for anything if we don't give back in return?

Many years ago, when I was a Christian but did not fully understand tithing, I remember placing money in the offering plate if all our bills were paid and we had a bit extra. I'd usually throw in a few ones or maybe a five, and on good weeks I'd drop in ten, thinking I had done something great.

Keep in mind, I was in my mid-twenties and had not been married long, with a very young child and a new double-wide trailer.

At this time, my husband was working on a garbage route, I was a manager in a card shop, and our bills were almost more than we could bear.

It was Christmas time and I had spent the day cleaning the house while my husband was working, and our only child, a daughter, played with her toys. It was her very first Christmas, and I so wanted to make it special for her. I put up my artificial Christmas tree, but I had no decorations to speak of.

I was heartbroken trying to figure out a way to decorate our tiny tree, so my little girl would understand what Christmas was all about.

Now, let me pause there a moment and make you see that even though I had been a Christian for fourteen years, I didn't really have a clue what Christmas was all about. Sure, I knew it was Jesus' birthday and it was all about Him, but deep in my heart I was still stuck on Christmas trees and bright lights. Boy, did I have a lot to learn.

I went to our checkbook and looked to see what our balance was. If my calculations were right, we had twenty dollars, and that was it until the next payday.

I threw down my checkbook and questioned God. Why were we struggling so much? Why didn't He bless us as I'd seen Him bless so many others? All I needed was Christmas decorations. Was that too much to ask?

Yes, I know, I was sounding a bit selfish, right? I didn't take into consideration that we had a beautiful home, I had the most adorable little girl, and my husband and I both had jobs. It wasn't God's fault that our debt was so high; we had gotten ourselves into that.

As I was sulking and complaining to God, my aunt knocked on my door. I smiled and invited her in.

She explained to me that she was going through the neighborhood taking up money for a family down the street that I knew very well. He had been laid off from his job and they had three young children, and she wanted to present them with money to help them through Christmas and perhaps buy a few gifts for their children.

As I was listening to her tell me their dilemma, my mind went to the twenty dollars we had in our bank account. How could I tell my aunt that I didn't have any extra money to be giving away when I couldn't even afford to buy decorations for our tree?

In my mid-twenties, I still had much to learn about hearing the voice of God, but I know it was the Holy Spirit who told me to write her a check for twenty dollars.

I wrote out the check, telling her I was sorry I couldn't do more. She thanked me and said that would help more than I knew, and that she was not going to tell who gave what. She would just write one huge check from the neighborhood.

After she left, I questioned God again. Why did I do that? I just gave every last cent we had until payday. What was I thinking?

Within fifteen minutes after my aunt had gone, I heard another knock on my door. When I opened it, there stood our neighbor down the street who had lost his job—the one my aunt was taking up the money for. He was carrying a huge box in his hands.

He laughed and said, "Forgive me for bringing you our leftovers from Christmases past, but the children have decided to make homemade decorations this year to go on the tree, and I have so many things I won't be able to use. Please don't think I'm crazy, but God placed you on my heart, and so I thought you might need these."

When he handed me the box and I opened it up, I gasped out loud and started crying uncontrollably. He placed his arms around me, and asked if I was all right, explaining that they were just old lights and decorations; it was nothing to cry over, really.

How could I tell him what had been going through my mind all day? How could I tell him that I had just given his family my last twenty dollars? He had no idea at that moment money was being collected on his behalf, and here he was blessing me when he had so little.

I learned something valuable that day that changed my whole life. First of all, you can't out give God. God really does hear every prayer we pray, and He loves us more than we can ever imagine.

God knew I was still young and had a lot to learn. All I asked for were Christmas lights and decorations, and not only did He bless me with the things I asked for, He sent them to me through the man I had just blessed.

****

By rights, 10% percent of our gross belongs to God. We are to honor Him by giving Him His share, and He holds us accountable when we don't.

****

Give, and it will be given to you. Good measure, pressed down, shaken together, running over will be poured into your lap. For with the measure you use, it will be measured to you. (Luke 6:38) NIV

****

Our offerings come after our 10%. Remember 10% is required; it is what He expects each of us to do. Our offerings are when we give more than our 10%, and that is when He truly blesses us, because we let go of what was ours just to bless others.

How can we ask God for anything if we don't give to Him in return, just like the Christmas lights and decorations? When I was willing to let go of all I had at that moment, He gave me back just what I asked for. He really is amazing like that.

He blesses others through our giving and blesses us through their giving; that's just the way it works. He can do nothing without a willing vessel ready to give and to serve others.

****

When I was in my late twenties, I was becoming more of a prayer warrior and learning to hear the voice of God more clearly. By this time, I had two daughters who were both young, and my husband worked night shift.

One night I was praying and telling God to use me. On this particular night, He pressed upon my heart to call my uncle who lived with my grandmother at the time, and tell him that He was robbing God.

I was very confused. My uncle had not been on my mind all day, and I didn't understand why God wished me to call him now at nine o'clock at night.

The feeling I was having kept getting stronger, and I knew I had promised God that I would do whatever he commanded of me. So, taking a deep breath, I picked up the phone to call my uncle, who I prayed was still up.

He answered the phone and seemed pleased to hear from me, stating that he never went to bed before midnight.

My uncle, to my knowledge, had never been a church-going man. He had been single all of his life, and had no children. Everyone in the family knew if they ever needed any money, he was the man to get a loan from, because he had no bills except to help my grandmother with the utilities.

Shakily, I told him that God had placed him on my heart and wanted me to give him a message.

He listened carefully as I explained that I didn't understand what the message meant, but that He had told me through my spirit that he was robbing God, and that I was supposed to tell him this.

He grew very quiet for a moment, and then thanked me for calling.

Never again did he ask me about this from then until he passed away years later. I'm still not sure if he knew what God was trying to tell him, but I like to think it had something to do with his tithes, and after that, my uncle did his fair share. At least, I had done what God wanted of me.

****

Remember this: whoever sows sparingly will also reap sparingly, and whoever sows generously will also reap generously. Each man should give what he has decided in his heart to give, not reluctantly or under compulsion, for God loves a cheerful giver.

(2 Corinthians 8:6-8)NIV

****

God delights when we give to others and give more than we are required to give. Anytime someone asks me to pray for their financial blessings, I always ask them if they are faithful with their tithing. I am much bolder now and not afraid to ask. Besides, tithing is so important they need to understand that to ask God for a financial blessing would be very selfish if they never gave Him what He asks for in return.

Remember, if He cannot trust you with little, then it is possible little is all you will ever have.

The church I attend ran numbers to see how many members paid tithes faithfully, and found that only 47% of all the church members pay tithes faithfully.

This blew my mind, thinking that less than half the families that attended church gave to God what was rightfully His, while the rest held back and decided God didn't need their money.

I don't want to face God someday and have Him tell me that I robbed Him, or have my phone ring some night and have someone else tell me that He was sending me a message that I was robbing Him.

Think of all God did for you! Just getting up in the morning is a blessing. He came to this earth and wrapped Himself in flesh and died for all of us.

Someone had to make payment for you, and Jesus made that payment on the cross. God wants to profit for giving you life. He wants to bless others through you and bless you through them.

Today is the day to start, with the very next paycheck, and give God what is God's by giving to the storehouse (your church or a church you support).

Chapter Sixteen

Let the Dead Bury the Dead
Letting go of toxic friends

****

Do not be yoked together with unbelievers. For what do righteousness and wickedness have in common? Or what fellowship can light have with darkness? *(2 Corinthians 6:14) NIV*

****

There is nothing more miserable than to be around someone who is always miserable. You know what I am talking about, those people who are always causing trouble and drama wherever they go.

Some people just aren't happy unless they are miserable, and they love to see you miserable, too.

Some people will never be happy with your success because deep inside they are jealous of you and can't understand why they are in the slump they are in and will never realize they do most of it to themselves.

Some people love to create drama and cause trouble to get attention. People who hunger for attention will get attention any way possible, even if it's bad.

Some people are like poison that Satan uses, and they don't even realize it.

****

I once had a friend that I loved with all my heart. If you remember the story I told you about me growing up shy and feeling ugly, then you will know why I was happy just to have a friend I could hang out and do things with.

We grew up together and spent many nights at each other's house. Her family had money and my family was poor.

I remember one Christmas when she was at my home visiting, she looked under our tree and laughed and said, "Is that all the presents you have?"

I laughed it off.

After Christmas, she showed me her very expensive fur coat and asked what Santa had brought me. To this day, I will never remember what it was Santa brought, but I do remember her laughing and saying I guess your dad couldn't afford as much as mine.

One day we were getting ready to go somewhere at her home, and she looked into the mirror and said, "It's too bad you're not as pretty as I am."

I again laughed it off.

As we grew older, it seemed that she was never happy unless she was creating some sort of conflict between us or someone else. She seemed to love misery because it followed her wherever she went.

So many times I would jump when she hollered and try to please her, even as adults, until one day she became angry at me because I was busy working and not spending enough time with her, and she said some pretty hateful and hurtful things to me.

After so many years of childhood friendship and on into an adult friendship, I decided to forgive her, but to wipe my feet and walk away.

There were just too many years of strife, and I no longer needed that for my life.

****

Do not give what is holy to the dogs; nor cast your pearls before swine, lest they trample them under their feet, and turn and tear you to pieces. (Matthew 7:6) NKJV

****

It's okay to let friends go when they cut you down or cause stress in your life. To live a life pleasing to God, you must remove yourself from the drama that others cause and walk away.

Sometimes letting go of a friend who has been with us throughout most of our life is one of the hardest things we can do, but it is sometimes necessary to be a servant of God.

This also holds true with family members or ex-spouses. If they are not living a life pleasing to God, and are dragging you down with them, then it's necessary to cut them loose from your life.

This doesn't mean to be rude or hateful to them, because there may come a time you have to witness to them. If you are able to hear the voice of God, then He will guide you and you will know when the time is right.

What I mean is to pull away and distance yourself from them. Staying around someone who is like poison to you will eventually kill you spiritually.

No matter how hard you may try, you cannot drag someone close to God; they have to be willing to take the steps themselves.

You can encourage and let your light shine for God, but if you have tried multiple times and they are still living a life of sin, cut the rope and walk away.

As hard as you try to bring them closer to God, they could very well pull you back to evil. You have to be a very strong Christian to be able to turn away from temptation, so it's best to keep yourself surrounded with other believers who are trying to also live a Christlike life.

It's crucial for a young believer to stay away from toxic people, especially if you have ever suffered from an addiction and are now free from it. It takes years to be able to say no and walk away from the things you were addicted to; even if you feel certain you would never do it again, Satan has a way of luring you in when you hang with the wrong people long enough.

It's okay not to trust yourself; it's better to be safe than sorry.

So many teenagers who have been raised in church and taught the ways pleasing to God sometimes go off to college and find themselves surrounded by unbelievers who are constantly offering them things of the world. Because they desire to fit in, they try it and then it escalates from there. The body is willing, but the flesh is weak.

Don't ever get to the point where you feel you are invincible, and that there is just no way you could stray. Trust me, there is no one at this point, because there is no one who has ever lived a sinless life but Christ, and we are far from Him and His goodness.

****

One of the biggest traps we can fall into is believing that God placed another man or woman in our life of the opposite sex if we are married.

Perhaps our marriage is less than perfect and we feel we have made the wrong decision when we look at our spouse. Then out of the blue, bam, here comes this other person that in our hearts we are sure was sent straight from God. After all, He wants us to be happy, right?

As I stated in chapter eight, God will never send another person to a married man or woman. Trust me; I had to learn this the hard way.

The grass isn't always greener on the other side, and if you start to think that maybe it is, then you need to fertilize your own lawn.

So many people make the mistake of secretly talking to another man or woman, thinking that the communication is so much better. It starts off with small talk, and then leads to heavy conversation, where you find yourself agreeing to meet somewhere out of town so no one will know. All the while, you think it's innocent because nothing is wrong with just having lunch and talking.

Lunch turns into dinner, and you find yourself agreeing to meet again or going to a motel room, because all of a sudden you think you're in love.

You tell yourself that you haven't been truly happy in years. Maybe you are in a loveless marriage where there is no intimacy and you hunger so badly for just a loving touch from someone who cares.

Satan is so good at convincing you that what you are about to do will be okay. Besides, if your spouse truly loved you, you certainly would never have found yourself here to begin with. Wrong!

There is a huge difference between love and lust. Ask yourself, do you really want to sleep with someone who knows you're married and doesn't care? What sort of person is this?

This sort of relationship is toxic to you, and trust me, nothing good will come out of it whatsoever, because God will never bless it to begin with.

If you find yourself falling for this trap, look deeply at your spouse. Go back in your mind to when you first met. You were so happy and in love, or you would not have gotten married to begin with.

Maybe the problem you are having isn't just them. Maybe it has a lot to do with you also. Sure, they have changed, but trust me, so have you.

Are you still the loving, fun person you used to be, or have you fallen into a rut that you just can't seem to crawl out of?

Stop waiting for them to change back, and be willing to make the first move. Tell them how much you appreciate them and how beautiful or handsome they are. It doesn't matter if they've gained a few pounds or their hair is grey, they are still the same person you vowed to live your life with.

Maybe the reason they don't act as if they care anymore is because you stopped caring yourself.

Seek Christian marriage counseling if you need to, but don't be so quick to give up. By all means, stay away from the person you are enticed by, because nothing good can come of it, if you are already married to someone else.

****

It doesn't take a rocket scientist to know which friends or acquaintances are toxic for our well-being. Use your head, not your heart. God will lead you in the right direction.

Chapter Seventeen

Relationship Do's and Don'ts

****

Then the Lord said, "It is not good that man should be alone; I will make him a helper fit for him." *(Genesis 2:18)NIV*

****

What a great chapter to end with, especially since we just finished the last one and can move right along into relationships.

When God created Adam, He saw right away that it was not good for man to be alone, so God created a helper fit for him, a beautiful woman, who, I am sure, left Adam breathless.

Since the beginning of time, God intended for marriage to be between man and woman. He created them this way so they could reproduce. Wasn't God a genius? Have you ever really thought about that?

The problem with the world is we don't always wait on God to choose the one fit for us; we seem to think we are great at picking them out ourselves. After all, no one knows what we need more than us, right? Wrong!

Since we know God's Word tells us we need to be equally yoked, many have misunderstood and thought it meant equally raced, but the truth is equally yoked means a Christian should marry another Christian. Very seldom do marriages work when only one member of the marriage unit is a believer and the other isn't.

****

Furthermore, you shall not intermarry with them; you shall not give your daughters to their sons, nor shall you take their daughters for your sons. (Deuteronomy 7:3) NIV

****

We are the human race, all of us, no matter what color our skin may be. God doesn't care what the color of your skin is, as long as you don't marry an animal or someone of the same sex. After all, Moses married Zipporah, a dark-skinned, Cushite woman and Moses was a Hebrew.

Nowhere in God's Word does it say that a man and woman have to be the same color, just that marriage is between a man and woman, and they must be equally yoked.

When God looks at us, He doesn't see the color of our skin, but the kindness of our heart and whether He has a relationship with us.

I've often wondered if God made us different colors just to see how we treated each other.

****

As a woman who has been married more than once, I can tell you that I haven't always waited on God.

Like most people, the euphoric feeling you have when you first meet someone new is enough to convince us we are in love.

A simple kiss leaves us spellbound, and we think, beyond a shadow of a doubt, they are the one God sent just for us.

The truth is, Satan too, can place people in your path, and they may not be good for you at all.

Right after my ex-husband left me, I dated a man for a while who did not believe that Jesus was the Messiah. He was born and raised in Iran, and even though he was not Muslim, he wasn't a Christian either.

I knew better, but I was convinced that this very kind man only needed guidance, and I was just the one to guide him, or so I thought.

We dated for six straight months, and even though I bought him a Bible and tried my best to convince him that Jesus was God in the flesh sent here to die for our sins, he just laughed and told me I was crazy.

I finally realized I was in a dead-end relationship that was leading me nowhere, and so I broke it off.

Three days later, after crying my eyes out over a man who didn't even believe in Jesus, I met the man I am married to today. A lot can happen in just three days.

Jim is not only a believer, but has been a Christian since he was only six years old. He has done many mission trips and has stayed very involved with a church all throughout his life.

Do we argue? Of course we do, but we have learned through other failed marriages that the most important thing in a marriage is putting God first, even above each other.

We both are deeply rooted in a Bible-believing church that preaches the whole word and not just part of it. We are both small-group leaders and enjoy fellowshipping with our group every other Tuesday night.

We pray together, not only with our group, but with each other as husband and wife.

Since we both have baggage from failed marriages, sometimes that baggage finds its way into our marriage today and we tend to get aggravated over things that shouldn't bother us.

Thank goodness we both love each other enough that our love stays strong, and we always manage to work out our differences.

When you are married, each day is a process of give and take. You may have heard it said marriage is 50/50, but that isn't true. A great marriage is when each of you gives 100%.

God commands us to love each other, and we always make sure that not one day goes by that we don't tell the other just that.

We both agree that divorce will never be an option for us. We are going to grow old together and love each other through every struggle we may face.

****

The Lord God made woman from the rib He had taken out of man. The man said, "This is now bone of my bone and flesh of my flesh. She shall be called woman, for she was taken out of man." That is why man leaves his father and mother and is united to his wife, and they shall become one flesh. *(Genesis 2:22-24)NIV*

****

I don't know about you, but I pray for my marriage daily. Each of us likes to think it's the other's fault when we argue, when most of the time we are both at fault.

I have written out a prayer that is great to pray when your marriage is having problems.

****

Lord, heal our marriage, and let the healing start with me.

Have mercy on me Lord, a wife who has failed so often to demonstrate Your love.

Teach me to love Jim the way You love each of us, and help me to understand the baggage he may still carry from past relationships as You help him to understand mine. Help us both with that baggage and to be able to forgive and let it go.

Teach me to be a vessel of Your love, Your joy, Your peace, with patience and kindness and gentleness.

Show me how to love in such a way that he is inspired to praise You!

Glorify Yourself in me.

Amen

Why not start today to make up your own prayer, or feel free to use mine and start praying for your marriage. After all, your spouse is supposed to come after God and before your children, so having a great marriage is crucial for living a Godly life.

****

If you are single and looking for that perfect mate, I have some news for you that you may not want to hear. You can search the world over and will never find that person, because no one is perfect. There will always be things about them that you're not going to like, even if it's something as small as their making a noise when they chew their food.

Even though you will never find anyone who's perfect, there are a few things you have to ask yourself before committing yourself to this person for life.

1. Are they a Christian, or do they just say they are? Can you tell by the way they live their life, or is it questionable?

2. Do they respect their parents? Or do they disobey them and talk badly about them behind their back?
3. Is this person you are dating someone you would want to wake up beside for the rest of your life? If you know in your heart they are not husband or wife material, then you are wasting your time, and time is too valuable to waste.
4. Would this person make a great mother or father? Remember, they will help raise your children.
5. Do they have any bad habits that really drive you crazy? Or do you think you can convince them to give it up after you are married. (Trust me, you can't.)
6. Have you ever been in an argument, and if so, how did they handle it? If they have fits of rage, run while you have the chance!
7. If you already have children from a previous marriage, how do they treat them? Do they treat them like their own, or do they make it obvious that they want no part of them?
8. Do they serve you when they have the opportunity, or do they always expect you to serve them?
9. Are they easy to talk to, or does it take an act of congress to get them to pay attention when it's something that is really important?
10. Would they rather be in church with you or partying with their friends?

Trust me, you are not going to change them. They are who they are, and if you can't accept who they are, then move on.

****

My husband tells our younger children they can date when they are ready to get married. I laugh when I see his fourteen-year-old daughter and my fifteen-year-old son when they look at him as if he must be kidding. (We have ten children between us.)

If you think about it, he really is on to something. How many teenagers date when they are too young emotionally to be able to handle a relationship?

Teenage pregnancies run rampant in America, with the majority being allowed to date even as early as thirteen. 33,000 abortions are performed every day, and most of those are performed on teenagers who are still babies themselves.

It is so important to teach your children abstinence and honoring God with their body and waiting for sex until after marriage. Their body is a temple of God and not to be given away to just anyone, but only to the man or woman God has chosen for them.

Teaching them what to look for in a husband and wife at an early age will set the stage for a good future.

And again, if the person you are dating is not someone you would want to marry, then why are you wasting your time?

I learned the hard way that the only man I truly need is God. Yes, I love my husband with all my heart, but serving God is the most important thing in my life. It hasn't always been that way, though, and that's why I have had so much heartache in my life; if only I'd known then what I know now.

****

Thank goodness the past is the past and today is a brand-new day just waiting to explore the possibilities with God in the lead....to love Him....to serve Him....to be a better you. Go after it; God is waiting and eager to get started blessing others through you TODAY!

A letter from Karen.......

*****

I enjoyed writing this book, my first attempt at nonfiction. I hope it has touched you and led you closer to Christ.

I can't stress enough how important it is to know God's Word. If you do not have a Holy Bible because you cannot afford one, please send me an email and leave your address, and I will be happy to mail you one free of charge.....it is ***that*** important to me.

In fact, I would love to hear from you if this book touched you in any way or helped you. I would love to talk to you and pray with you.

For speaking engagements, please allow at least six weeks advance notice.

****

You can email me at:
Karenyp46@gmail.com
Web Address: www.sbpra.com/KarenAyers
Facebook: Karen Ayers, Author, Motivational Speaker
Also find me on: Twitter and LinkedIn

****

Other Books Written By Karen Ayers:
The Secrets of Westingdale
Sweet Summer Rain

Review Requested:

If you loved this book, would you please provide a review at Amazon.com?

CPSIA information can be obtained
at www.ICGtesting.com
Printed in the USA
LVHW041327300323
742972LV00004B/212

9 781681 816975